The Refinery

Overcoming Drug Addictions
Through The Supernatural Power
Available to You

Featuring

The **Refinement** Process

Ronald Gibson

The Refinery - Overcoming Drug Addictions Through The Supernatural Power Available to You

Copyright © 2016 Ronald Gibson

ISBN: 978-0-9962448-0-0

Published by Center Cross Creations
PO Box 90358, Rochester, NY 14609

www.TheRefinementProcess.com

No part of this book may be reproduced, stored in a retrieval system or transmitted in any form or by any means - electronic, mechanical, photocopy, recording or any other - except for brief quotations, without permission in writing from the publisher.

Unless otherwise indicated, all dictionary definitions are taken from the online version of Merriam-Webster Dictionary, An Encyclopedia Britannica Company

Unless otherwise indicated, all Scripture is taken from the King James Version of the Holy Bible.
Scripture marked NKJV is taken from the New King James Version. Copyright 1982 by Thomas Nelson, Inc. Used by permission. All rights reserved.
Scripture marked NIV is taken from the New International Version. Copyright 1973, 1978, 1984, 2011 by Biblica, Inc. Used by permission. All rights reserved worldwide.
Scripture marked NASB is taken from the New American Standard Bible. Copyright 1960, 1962, 1963, 1968, 1971, 1972, 1973, 1975, 1977, 1995 by The Lockman Foundation. Used by permission.
Scripture marked NLT is taken from the New Living Translation. Copyright 1996, 2004, 2007 by Tyndale House Publishers, Inc. Used by permission, All rights reserved.

First Edition: January 2016
10 9 8 7 6 5 4 3 2 1

Please note that Center Cross Creations publisher's style capitalizes certain pronouns in Scripture that refer to the Father, Son, and the Holy Spirit. Boldface type in the Scripture quotations indicates the author's emphasis.

Copy Edited by Alice Gissendanner & Sonya Haynes
Edited by Rebecca Chalone
Interior Design by Custom-book-tique
Cover Design by Mary Tes

Printed in the United States of America

CONTENTS

ACKNOWLEDGMENTS 7
DEDICATION 9
PREFACE 11
    The Supernatural Power Available To You 13
INTRODUCTION 15
    Kids At Play – Going Astray 15
    The Journey Starts With One Step 16
    Down, Down, Down 16
    Wheeling and Dealing 18
    How Low Can You Go? 20
    Gone With The Wind 21
    Marva's Story 22
    A Date with Destiny 24
THE REFINERY 27
    The Refinement Process 28
    The Staging Areas 28
    The Stations 29
    The Review Platforms 29
    Recovery versus Refinement 29
STAGING AREA ONE 33
THE REFLECTION STATION 35
    My Story 35
    You are the Person in the Mirror 37
    The Search Begins Now 37

Action Step 1 37
Reflection, Your Starting Point for Refinement 38
Let's Face it 40
Action Step 2 41
Refinement Hero 43

REFLECTION REVIEW PLATFORM 47
STAGING AREA TWO 49
THE REPENTANCE STATION 51
Standing at the Crossroads 51
The Refiner 53
Not Religion, It's About Relationship 53
Change Your Mind; Change Your Life 57
Action Step 57
You Need a Course Correction 58
Refinement Hero 59
My Story 60
What You Must Do to be Refined 61

REPENTANCE REVIEW PLATFORM 65
STAGING AREA THREE 67
THE REDEMPTION STATION 69
Kidnapped and Held For Ransom 69
Free Delivery, Paid In Full 70
God loved you first. God loved you best. 72
God loved you completely 72
What Does He See When He Looks At Me 72
Action Step 1 73

    My Story 74

    Your Believer and Your Thinker 76

    Release and Relief 78

    The Regina Goethe Story 79

    The Boy Who Lost His Boat 84

    Action Step 2 85

REDEMPTION REVIEW PLATFORM 87

STAGING AREA FOUR 89

THE RECOMMITMENT STATION 91

    My Story 91

    Stay on Course – Stay Committed 92

    Horizontal and Vertical Commitments 93

    Vowing a Vow 95

    Action Step 1 97

    Refinement Hero 98

    My Story 99

    Stay Perfected – Stay Pure 101

    Action Step 2 102

RECOMMITMENT REVIEW PLATFORM 105

STAGING AREA FIVE 107

THE REEMERGENCE STATION 109

    Refinement Hero 109

    Out of the Cocoon 111

    Visibility Restored 111

    Control Your Environment 112

    Polluted Pressures 113

    Polluted People 114

    Polluted Paraphernalia..115

    Action Step 1 116

    My Story 117

    Successful Living Through Refinement............................118

    Action Step 2 120

    The Rose Goode Story...121

    The Refiner's Benefit Package 126

REEMERGENCE REVIEW PLATFORM.................................129

RELAPSE ROAD 131

    My Story 132

    Sign Posts on Relapse Road 134

    Triggers, Traps, Temptations and Triumphs....................136

    Curiosity Killed the Cat, It Can Harm You Too.............136

    Action Step 137

    False Justifications 138

    The Craig Gause Story...139

    Fallen, But Not Flattened 143

RECOMMENDATIONS TO AVOID RELAPSE ROAD..............145

WELCOME TO YOUR NEW LIFE..147

    The Ricky Snell Story 147

WARNINGS FOR YOUR NEW LIFE..153

    My Story 153

ENDNOTES 157

Acknowledgments

My heart beats in sync with the heart of my dearest friend and lover, Marva. Next to Christ she is my greatest hero. Their love rescued me. I will love her until death eventually causes us to part.

    Bishop Gregory L. Parris and Pastor Myra Parris for their priceless leadership and friendship; Thank you for your loving-kindness and your faithfulness to me through all my generations.

    Bishop Paul Parnell and First Lady Myrtle Parnell for their ageless wisdom; Thank you for always believing in me and my vision for ministry. Thank you for being my wise counselors and friends.

    Ricky Snell, Rose Goode, Regina Goethe and Craig Gause for the courage to share their stories of drug addiction. Thank you for your transparency. I hope your stories inspire hope in all who read them.

    Alice Gissendanner, Sonya Haynes and Rebecca Chalone for their devotion to this project and the many hours they spent in the editing of this book. Thank you all.

    I would especially like to thank all those who contributed to this book in so many other ways.

DEDICATION

As a little boy I loved to clomp around in my father's size 10 shoes. The years passed and I grew up. Now my shoe size is 12, and yet I still could never fill my father's shoes (although I continue to try).

I am amazed by how the things I accomplish in my life reflect his accomplishments.

His life was complemented and colored by his best friend and lover, my mother. She is the one who kept him on the straight and narrow path. Their love evolved and their marriage endured the tests of time.

I dedicate this book to the memory of my dad Benjamin H. Gibson, Sr. and to the delight in still having the hugs and kisses of my mom Elsie A. Gibson.

Preface

It is the function of perfection to make one know one's imperfection. Augustine

Throughout history gold has been the standard whereby wealth is measured. The ancient kingdoms of Ethiopia, Egypt, Babylon, Greece, and Rome each associated this metal with power and prestige. In these kingdoms, gold was not accumulated in stockpiles; it was acquired to be displayed and seen. Whether fashioned into royal thrones or crowns, elaborate jewelry or dinnerware, a man or woman's possession of gold symbolized their elevated status.

Gold in its natural state is not so beautiful. The finished artistry of the goldsmith requires the arduous process of refinement. Gold is an ore which is a mixture of iron, silver, or other metals. The purification of gold involves the removal of those other metals. This gold refinement process is known as parting, metallurgy, or alchemy.

In ancient Greece, gold was retrieved from the rivers and streams where it was found in the sand. Prospectors would spread sheepskins on the rocks of the river beds. Next, they would pour the gold-rich sand over the sheepskin, letting the water wash away the sand. The heavier gold would get trapped in the wool (you might remember the tale of the Golden Fleece). But even with this method of prospecting, there had to be a process for refinement.

Several gold refinement processes evolved over the centuries, but it really "boiled down" to either a solid-state method or a chemical method. One early solid-state method involved the combination of the gold ore, salt, clay pottery shards, and urine. This mixture went in to the caldron which was then fired, skimmed, and cooled multiple times. The impurities in the gold formed chlorides and those insoluble salts were removed from the molten metal by skimming the surface. With each firing, skimming and cooling, the gold was refined to a purer state.

Along with those solid-state refinement methods, there arose chemical methods. In fact, the earliest dawning of the science of chemistry was centered on the study of the properties of gold and how to draw it out of base metals. This was referenced in the scholarly writings of nineteenth century chemist and gold assayer Sir Thomas Kirke Rose. In his 1898 book, *The Metallurgy of Gold*, he wrote, "From the fourth to the fifteenth century, chemistry, which was first called 'chemia', and then 'alchemy,' was defined as the art of transmuting base metals into gold and silver. Almost all scientific pursuit during that time was directed toward that desire. After that, chemistry took on a new goal. Its new aim was the investigation of the composition of drugs and their effect on the human body."

Alchemy, the futile attempt to turn base metal into gold, which led to the true science of ore refinement, later evolved into pharmacology, the science of drugs. I find it fascinating that the science of gold refinement led to our modern science of drug production. Ironically, because of the misapplication and misuse of drugs (pharma), which has led to an epidemic of drug addictions, there is great need for the evolution of methods to effectively refine the human spirit. Today, many people are in desperate need for soul refinement, which can include the rescue of a precious human soul from drug addictions.

Whereas gold, in its natural state, is not very beautiful; the human spirit, in its natural state, is not beautiful. The beauty of the finished gold requires a process of refinement; likewise, the raw human spirit needs to be refined. The purification of gold involves the removal of other base metals. The refinement of the human spirit involves the removal of impurities such as bad habits, immoralities, and addictions.

The human spirit left untreated, might lead a person into difficulties in areas of loving relationships, good physical and mental health, stable personal finances, and the attainment of short and long term goals.

The refinement of the human spirit is the basis for the book you now hold. **The Refinery, Overcoming Drug Addictions Through The Supernatural Power Available To You**, will take you on a life changing process of spiritual refinement. True, this Refinery is not a brick and mortar building, but it is the internal space where your soul can be rescued and refined.

The Supernatural Power Available To You

Supercomputer, Supersize, Supernova, Superhero, Superstar, Superhuman, Supermarket, Super Bowl - we use the word *super* so often as a descriptor that it has become common. But, there is nothing common about anything that is super. Super is so far removed from common that they are not even in the same league. The word super is synonymous with ultra, enhanced, augmented or elevated; superior or supreme. So how do we associate *super* with *nature* and arrive at supernatural?

The term nature is used in reference to the world around us. Many people attribute earthly forces and occurrences to *Mother Nature*. Nature encompasses the physical forces with which we live (the laws of nature). This concept of nature applies not only to the external world, but it also describes our inner being (human nature). This includes human instincts, tendencies, drives, appetites and character traits.

Supernatural combines that which is super and that which is nature. It does not change nature; instead, it interrupts and interferes with nature because it works on a higher plain. Therefore the results achieved through the supernatural far surpass what could be achieved naturally. This combination of super with nature results in power; it is synergy, a dynamic which is greater than the sum of the two parts (super + nature). It is an extreme enablement which operates beyond the limitations of nature.

Super-nature is the "over and above". It is what we refer to as "outside the normal." Super-nature exceeds the earthly physics of time, space, speed, or matter (substance). And yet, super-nature can be used to affect our physical world in ways that cannot be fully understood or explained.

Nature is beyond mankind's control. Man cannot command the sun or moon; he cannot direct the rain or snow. Man cannot control the mighty wind, the raging rivers, or the powerful ocean tides. Nevertheless, he can harness these powerful forces for his benefit. Sailing ships, hydroelectric dams, and wind turbines are some examples of countless ways in which man harnesses nature and uses it beneficially.

Super-nature can also be is used to affect your inner world; your character, appetites and drives.

In **The Refinery, Overcoming Drug Addictions Through The Supernatural Power Available To You**, you will discover that you can have access to divine super-nature. You will see that it can be used to overcome and rid yourself of unhealthy human tendencies, character issues, bad habits as well as addictions. Just like nature, you cannot command or control super-nature. However, you can access the dynamic force of super-nature, which can forever improve your life. You, too, can overcome drug addictions through the supernatural power available to you.

I invite you to take the journey with me through The Refinery.

Introduction

"Hey, Baby, I got a couple joints. Let's get high." I said to my friend Marva.

Little did I know that when I made that statement the course of my life would be forever changed. Those ten words set in motion a transformation that is nothing short of miraculous.

I was being radically positioned for **The Refinement Process**!

Kids At Play – Going Astray

Getting high began for me when I was a teenager. Growing up in a small upstate New York town, life was predictable. Too predictable! For a fifteen year old kid, that meant BORING!

I needed something, anything that could jazz-up my *Leave It to Beaver* life. I found that special something at the counter of the neighborhood pharmacy. I started my journey to drug addiction with a bottle of codeine cough syrup.

On Friday nights, several of us guys would each "develop a cold" which would require medication. No simple cough drops for us thrill seekers. We would go to Wayne's Pharmacy where each of us would buy a bottle of Romilar, a non-prescription codeine cough syrup.

"All you boys sick at the same time?" the pharmacist would ask.

"Yes, sir," we lied. "It must be some bug going around."

Each of us would leave with his own bottle of medicine. The only real sickness we had was boredom. We wanted a thrill. We wanted to get high. And off we went. We would gather in a friend's bedroom, unwrap our stash, and proceed to chug the contents of the bottle, the whole bottle. We'd laugh and joke around knowing that soon we would be on our way…our way up…way up! Twenty minutes later it would start with the familiar warmth in the pit of our stomachs. Then our faces would get hot, real hot! Within the hour we were flying high like kites in the wind.

The Journey Starts With One Step

That was the beginning. That's how I began my personal journey to full-blown drug addiction. A bottle of cough syrup! From there it led to smoking marijuana, which led to hashish, which led to amphetamines (speed), and to barbiturates (downers). They led to psychedelics (mescaline and LSD) and to opiates (morphine, cocaine, and heroin). At the depth of my drug addiction, there was nothing that I would turn down to get high. If I couldn't "toke" it (smoke), I'd drop it (ingest). If I couldn't drop it, I'd snort it (sniffing). If I couldn't snort it, I'd shoot it (skin-pop or mainline). One way or another, I was going to get high.

From the quiet streets of Canandaigua, NY, my drug habit took me to the mean streets of Boston, to the "far-out" Haight-Ashbury district in San Francisco, to the barrios of Los Angeles and Tucson, AZ. From college campuses all over this country to "shooting dens" in Harlem and Bedford-Stuyvesant, NY, every step was lower and lower, begging, borrowing and stealing along the way.

Down, Down, Down

My friend, Rice Moon, was a regular "partner in crime" during many of my years of drugging. I first met him on Revere Street on Boston's Beacon Hill. We were both musicians, which formed the basis for our friendship. Rice played the blues harmonica; my instrument was bass guitar. We were kindred spirits and we played together in several bands. These party bands were formed for the purpose of playing music, scoring chicks, and getting high; not necessarily in that order. We were never creative enough to write our own music; therefore our repertoire was based on covering popular rock, rhythm and blues, funk, and fusion music.

Before I met Rice Moon, I thought that I was a heavy drug user. Boy was I wrong! Rice took his drug use seriously. He had a voracious appetite for weed, booze, and especially junk. Up to that time I had avoided junk, but I was about to get my first initiation in to the wonderful world of heroin.

Rice and I were in New York City for a few weeks waiting on an inheritance that he was to receive. Most days were spent listening to and playing music or hanging out with his cousins. I was never one for standing around on the corner, but that was their main function in life, hanging out and getting high. Each day Rice's hunger for heroin became more apparent. Finally, he could stand it no longer. We had to make a run to Bedford-Stuyvesant to score.

I'd seen some seedy sections of many big cities, but nothing could prepare me for Bed-Sty. Rice's cousins took us to the worst block in the hood. There, Rice found what he was looking for, a shooting den, a place for buying and shooting up heroin with other degenerates. Rice and I copped our stash and waited for our turns to use the one and only hypodermic needle in the house.

It was quite a scene. Guys sat around in various states of consciousness, from very anxious, those who were impatiently waiting their turn to shoot up, to very mellow, those who were already drifting off, embracing their euphoria. There were nine or ten other junkies in the place when the needle was passed to Rice. He knew the drill: place his rock in a beer-bottle lid, fire it up with your cigarette lighter until it cooks down into a smooth brown gravy, use the filter from your Newport or Marlboro, and place the tip of the needle on the filter to draw the liquid into the needle. That was when things got very bizarre and potentially dangerous.

Rice had already tied off his arm with his belt. While trying to fill the syringe, in his haste to shoot up, he pressed down much too hard on the needle and it broke. HE BROKE THE ONLY NEEDLE IN THE HOUSE! Most people would not understand the magnitude of this situation, unless you are, or were, a junkie.

The guys that had already shot up were oblivious to the situation; the junkie that noticed the broken needle was the next guy in line to shoot and he loudly raised holy hell in the place. Rice and I were in a real mess. Tempers flared and threats were leveled at us as we fled the scene fearing for our lives. We managed to escape (most junkies can't run very fast), but that was the last time I entered a shooting den.

Wheeling and Dealing

The use and abuse of drugs is very expensive. People resort to any means necessary to support their drug habit. I was no different. It occurred to me early on that I needed a daily flow of cash to pay for my daily flow of weed and narcotics. For me, the answer was to become a drug dealer.

There are many misconceptions concerning drug dealers. Hollywood movies sometimes portray the glamorous lifestyle of the big-time dealers: luxury cars, designer clothes, and plenty of cash. Or the movies go to the other extreme of characterizing the street corner pusher as a degenerate, preying on school children in the playground. Even though those extremes do exist in real life, most drug dealers fall somewhere between those two extremes, neither glamorous nor depraved.

My venture into the business of drugs started with dealing weed to my friends. It didn't take much smarts to realize that rather than consume a dime bag of weed and be out $10, I could buy two dime bags, twist-up five or six joints, sell them, and smoke up the profits for free. Those small-time nickel and dime transactions led to larger deals with much larger quantities.

My base of operations was Tucson, Arizona, where I lived and attended Pima College. I was a music major by day and a Rock musician on the weekends. That made for a ready market for my business endeavors. Tucson is not far from the U.S./Mexican border; therefore, the international trafficking of drugs was common. Being a student and a struggling musician, I didn't have the large amounts of cash needed to invest in the "product". For that reason, I became a "broker".

I had many social contacts ready to score, and I knew the guys bringing marijuana up from Mexico. My business model was simply to broker the deal by bringing the sellers and buyers together. I made a fee on each transaction. Generally, the fee was cash, but sometimes it was one or two kilos of weed. At my house it was not uncommon to have 2' x 2' x 4' bails of marijuana in my living room awaiting packaging and distribution.

One time, I brokered a deal between my supplier, Stan the Man, and some out-of-towners from the Midwest. They were going to buy kilos of pot to take home. They sampled Stan's stuff and were satisfied with the quality and price. The deal was set for two o'clock that afternoon at my place, where the guys were hanging out.

Tucson was a small, close-knit town, and word got around about the pending deal. Around noontime, Archie, another supplier that I knew, showed up at my door. He boasted about having some primo weed at a very low price, better than Stan's price. The guys wanted to try a sample. I was dead-set against it because of the pending deal; however, they were impatient and wanted to score quickly. It really didn't matter to me; I was going to make my profit regardless of whichever supplier they chose.

Archie really had some high quality weed. The buyers were convinced that his was the pot they wanted. Archie, wanting to make sure that the guys had enough cash, insisted that they show him their money, which they did. He said that he had the kilos in the trunk of his car and that he would go out and bring it in. He exited my house.

The next thing I knew, four masked men burst through the door with sawed-off shotguns and pistols drawn. They lined all of us up, facing the wall, with guns against the backs of our heads. The buyers were quickly relieved of almost $15,000. Archie and his boys fled the scene.

Miraculously, our vital bodily organs were still intact, not splattered on the wall in front of us. Many deals that go bad are not bloodless. That time, I dodged the bullet and thwarted death. Yet unknown to me, someone of a higher authority had other plans for my life.

How Low Can You Go?

Probably one of the lowest points on my journey was when my unconscious body was dumped in a gutter on a Boston street. Earlier that evening, I had walked down the outside stairs of the Commonwealth Avenue bar to meet some friends. It had been a long day of travel, so to unwind, I decided to have a couple of drinks. While getting drunk, the idea of taking some Quaaludes (a strong barbiturate), made sense to me. My body didn't agree.

The next day my friends told me that I was found passed-out on the floor of the bar. One of the bouncers carried me over his shoulder up the stairs and dumped me in the gutter of the street. A carful of thugs saw me as an easy mark for their lustful misdeeds. They tried to load my listless body into their vehicle. But my friend, Billy, persuaded the guys to load me into a cab instead. Billy whisked us away from the scene to his apartment, where I finally came-to the next afternoon. He rescued me from almost certain robbery, rape, and possibly murder!

Gone With The Wind

You would think that that incident would have been a wakeup call for me. Well, for most able-minded people that would have been enough. But, at that point, I couldn't be described as able-minded. In fact, drug abuse had left me feeble-minded. It is amazing to me, now, how desperate and devoid of good sense I had become.

Every druggie has a drug-of-choice, mine was cocaine. For me, marijuana was a mellow high, downers slowed me down too much, speed left me too jittery, and the psychedelics made me a little too spacey. Now, don't get me wrong, I would still do any and all of these drugs, but coke was my magic carpet ride. At that time, everyone I knew was doing it and everyone I knew had it. It didn't take long for my nose to acquire a real taste for it. Consequently, my body acquired a real craving for it. Coke was all the rage. Tragically, overdosings all too commonly occurred.

"Did you hear who OD'ed today?" was a typical question.

Hearing the person's name, the response was often, "Wow, I just saw him last night!"

"Well you won't see him anymore. He's dead."

Some friends died, and the rest of us were slowly dying. We just found ways of denying it to ourselves. The reality was that any one of us could take the very next overdose. We were losing friends way too quickly; it was either prison or the grave.

Another one bites the dust, it sounds very callous, but that was the way I thought back then. I didn't stop to consider that those buddies who died all had mothers, fathers, brothers, sisters, and other loved ones. I never stopped to consider the possibility of my father and mother, my siblings and loved ones looking down into my casket at my lifeless remains.

The one thing that I knew was that the finality of my friends' deaths was too much for me. I never attended any of their funerals. The thought of going to a funeral home or church and hearing a bunch of talk about the here-after was not for me.

Looking back, I think part of the thrill of cocaine was the risk involved in using it. It was almost like the risk that fools take playing Russian roulette: one bullet in one of the six chambers in the gun, spin the barrel, point it at your head, and pull the trigger. Either click, I survived, or BOOM, my brains are on the wall behind me. My mindset was reinforced by the tagline of a popular soft drink; *Things go better with Coke*.

Marva's Story

I first saw Marva at my sister Debby's wedding in Rochester, NY. At the time, I lived and worked in Boston. I took a week off from my taxi driving gig to attend the nuptials. It was great seeing family and friends. Marva really caught my eye at an after-party following the wedding reception. She was drop-dead gorgeous and I knew I had to make a play for her attention. We were introduced and we chatted briefly. She agreed to have dinner with me later that week. We had a good time, but I knew that soon I would be returning to my home in Boston. I needed to make my move.

Marva had a sunny personality. She was a joy to be around. She had a beaming smile, sparkling brown eyes, and a songlike laugh. Her brightness came from deep within her soul and radiated out like shafts of light. She was my beautiful beacon of love. When darkness surrounded me, Marva was my ray of hope that things would get better.

Although Marva was originally from Conway, South Carolina, she should have been born in Missouri, the *Show Me* state. She was a show me, prove it to me woman. For as long as I've known her, she has demonstrated an extreme level of compassion and loyalty. She was a very trusting person, but her trust came at a high price. When Marva trusted a person, it was generally not misplaced because that person had earned her trust. And that was my dilemma. I wasn't a trustworthy man.

Marva's issues with trust, or mistrust, came from early incidents when people who were closest to her failed to show themselves worthy to be trusted. As a teenager, her alcoholic father, whom she trusted, mentally and physically abused her. His vicious beatings were commonplace in her family. No one in her home escaped his unwarranted drunken rages. During one of those beatings, Marva fell and suffered a head concussion which resulted in a coma. She was hospitalized for weeks. Friends and family visited her. An attending nurse noticed that Marva rested peacefully except for when she heard her father's voice in the room. Then, she would become agitated.

Marva eventually recovered consciousness, but home life would never be the same. Her older, married sister, Jaunieta, rescued Marva and relocated her to her home in Rochester, NY. The move was just what she needed to make a full recovery both mentally and emotionally.

Marva finished high school and moved into her own apartment. She was always industrious and found good job opportunities. She had several boyfriends, but the relationships always ended over betrayed trust. She married Richard and settled down to raise a family. She had already had her first child, Melvin. Five years later, she had a daughter, Elizabeth. Unfortunately, the marriage was stormy and once again trust was at the center of the storm.

From time to time Richard would disappear, sometimes, for days or weeks. His longest disappearances were in the custody of the New York State Department of Corrections, where he served several terms. At least then Marva knew where he was. Other times, he would just stay away from their home. It all ended when she suffered a miscarriage. After she was discharged from the hospital, she returned home to find the apartment bare. Richard had abandoned her forever. He had taken everything and had left her to raise her two kids alone.

Months later, when I met Marva, she was newly divorced and raising her two young children without any other support from her ex-husband. That's tough, but she was making a good life for herself and her young family. Marva was always a *good girl*, having been raised by her God-fearing mother, Miriam. She wouldn't smoke, drink anything stronger than tea, cuss, or use strong language. She was truly a classy, intelligent, and beautiful woman. For me to pursue her, I felt out of my league. Plus, at first, she didn't know that I used drugs.

In the Bible, there is a story about a man who found a pearl of great value. He left and sold everything he owned, came back and bought the pearl.[1] For me, Marva was the valuable pearl. And she was available, but not for any fool with a song and a dance. She was available to this fool, me, if I would just forsake my foolish ways.

A Date with Destiny

Over the months to come, I frequently traveled to Rochester. My excuse was to see my family; however, my real intent was to see Marva. It was during one of those visits home, while out on a date, that I made the infamous statement, "Hey baby, I got a couple joints. Let's get high."

We were still just getting to know each other. There I was, a full blown drug addict, asking her to get high with me. At that time, I did not know that Marva had never used drugs. In fact, I don't think that she had ever even been drunk! She looked at me as if I had suddenly grown devil's horns and a pointy tail. She was horrified!

"You do that stuff?"

"Yeah, don't you?"

"No. I don't know anybody who does that!" she said.

At that point in my life, I didn't know anyone my age that didn't use drugs!

"Really?" I asked in amazement. I admitted, "I get high every day."

She simply told me, "Take me home."

She looked disappointed as she got out of the car and walked to her apartment. That was the end of our date that night, and it very well could have been the end of our friendship altogether. I was bewildered. I didn't understand; what was the big deal?

"I'll call her tomorrow," I thought, *"when she has calmed down. No big deal."*

The next day, when I called, she would not answer her phone. In fact, for that whole week she refused to see or to talk to me. It was as if I no longer existed. It was very frustrating because I really liked Marva. She was smart, witty, and very pretty. I was scheduled to return home to Boston in a few days, but, still, I couldn't get through to her.

Finally, on the day I was scheduled to leave town, I called, and she answered.

"Marva, this is Ron. Please, don't hang up!"

"Hi, Ron. What do you want?"

"I'm leaving today and I wanted to talk with you before I go."

"Well, talk." she coldly replied.

"What was the big deal the other night about getting high?" I asked.

I'll never forget her words.

She said, "Ron, you're a nice young man and I like you. But, I don't use drugs and I don't like being around people who use them. I don't want drugs in my life! So," she continued, "you can be with your drugs, or, you can be with me, but you can't have us both. You decide!" Then she hung up the phone.

My heart was troubled as I traveled back to Boston. I didn't know what to make of her statement. In fact, I was a little angry with her. I had never had a woman talk to me like that! Up until then, all the women I had dated had gotten high with me.

Who does she think she is, talking to me like that? I thought.

And yet there was something about Marva that gave me a glimpse at another way of living. There was a feeling that I had deep inside that my current life was shallow and aimless. Innately, I knew that Marva could be my last hope of a meaningful life, a drug-free life. Deep down within me I desired a change for the better.

These encounters with Marva set in motion a miraculous transformation in me. I did not realize it at the time, but I was being drawn into a life changing process. A process and change that would bring the answer for which I had hoped. By the end of the process, I was totally delivered from my drug addictions. The process worked for me, and I am convinced that it will work for you, too. I call it, **The Refinement Process**.

You will find more of my story as you take an amazing journey through a space I came to know as **The Refinery**.

The words printed here are concepts. You must go through the experiences.
Augustine

The Refinery

You don't change the old by resisting it; You change it by making it obsolete through superior methodology. Buckminster Fuller

A refinery is a dreadful place! The sights, the smells, the painful process of change can be overwhelming. The refinery is the place where raw metal ore is changed from corruptible to incorruptible, from impure to pure, from filthy to clean. The refinery cauldron is where the impurities are separated and removed from the raw metal ore. The refinery fire is a fearful place; however, the results are magnificent.

You are about to embark on a journey through a different kind of refinery. This is The Refinery of your body, soul and spirit. In this Refinery, you are like the raw metal ore. Just like the gold or silver refineries are for the removal of impurities, this Refinery is the space where *your* impurities will be removed. This Refinery is where you will go through **The Refinement Process**.

You will come to know the Director of Operations. I call him the Refiner. It was through His patient mastery and His personal sacrifice that I was delivered from drug addiction forever. Through autobiography, allegory, and action steps, I hope to lead you in a powerful transformation from a life enslaved to your drug addiction to a life of freedom.

I am not a doctor. I am not a clinical psychologist. I am just a man; a person just like you. I witnessed the miraculous power of The Refinery that forever changed me and forever changed my life. As a result of **The Refinement Process** I was finally FREE! My body, soul and spirit totally cleansed and made pure. That is what can happen to you in The Refinery.

The Refinement Process

Years ago, I worked with an addiction recovery ministry through my local church. There I counseled men and women who were hardcore drug addicts. Preparing to conduct counseling sessions, I looked back over my life and discovered the process that had brought about my deliverance from my years of drug addictions. I wrote down my discovery and used it as the basis for leading my weekly drug counseling sessions.

After years of living clean, free from drug addiction, I was able to share with my clients a more excellent way to become clean! I call it, **The Refinement Process**, and it all takes place in The Refinery.

Let's look at the floor plan of The Refinery to see the workflow. Just like any other refinery, the raw material is staged and made ready for each process, eventually emerging as a valuable finished creation. In this Refinery, there are five sequential processing lines each made up of a Staging Area, a Station and a Review Platform.

The Staging Areas

There are five Staging Areas. Before you can enter each Station, you must first go through the corresponding Staging Area. The Staging Areas are designed to prepare you for the process which awaits you in the next Station.

> Staging Area One will prepare you for the Reflection Station
> Staging Area Two will prepare you for the Repentance Station
> Staging Area Three will prepare you for the Redemption Station
> Staging Area Four will prepare you for the Recommitment Station
> Staging Area Five will prepare you for the Reemergence Station

The Stations

There are five Stations. Each Station is designed to move you in systematic progression from drug dependence to drug independence. This is where your hard work is accomplished. Each Station is a function of **The Refinement Process**.

> The Reflection Station – Seeing Present Reality
> The Repentance Station – Making a Directional Decision
> The Redemption Station - Restoring Ownership
> The Recommitment Station - Pledging Purity
> The Reemergence Station - Becoming Visible Again

The Review Platforms

After each Station there is a Review Platform. The Review Platforms are there to reinforce the main points of each Station. They serve as a place for inspection and quality assurance. In **The Refinement Process,** there is an orderly flow from the Staging Areas to the Stations to the Review Platforms.

Recovery versus Refinement

Many people have tried rehab centers to kick their drug addictions. Many have tried to maintain sobriety through 12-Step programs like AA or NA. If you are one of these people, and rehab or a 12-step program is working for you, I say GREAT. But, my research and personal experience has shown me that there are many people who try those methods and fail. There are alternative methods for eliminating addictions. **The Refinement Process** is a powerful alternative approach to living free from the grip of drug addiction.

There is no one-size-fits-all treatment. **The Refinement Process,** for many, is a more excellent way to achieve sobriety and live a healthier life. This is the process that worked for me and it has worked for others whom I have counseled. For those of you who are helpless and hopeless, there is help and there is hope.

Much of drug addiction treatment today is classified as *recovery treatment*. In The Refinery, you will find *refinement treatment*. Just what is the difference between recovery and refinement? Recovery is to find or get back something or someone who was missing or lost. Recovery is the process whereby something or someone is returned to a former status. But, what if that former status was horrible? What if that former status was dysfunctional? What if that former status was miserable? Generally, when people start abusing drugs, it is because something is either wrong or missing in their life. So, what exactly is being recovered? Horror? Dysfunction? Misery?

The Refinement Process is a purging and purifying methodology. The results: A complete and thorough purification of your spirit, soul, and body. Unlike a recovery methodology, **The Refinement Process** does not attempt to return you to a former status, rather, it guides you to become new and improved. The old impurities are removed; therefore, the end condition is far better than the former condition

Each human being is a unique individual person. You have your own personal victories and defeats, triumphs and tragedies, successes and failures. You have your own personal hopes, dreams, and desires, as well as, your own personal hurts, nightmares, and losses. **The Refinement Process** will work for each person; however, each person's reactions to the process will vary.

Generally, the length of time it takes to complete **The Refinement Process** is dependent upon your levels of acceptance and resistance. For some of you, your resistance is great. The greater the level of resistance, the slower the completion of the process. That means, the quicker you surrender to the processing, the quicker the completion of the process.

For some of you, **The Refinement Process** will work very quickly and completely. That is how it was for me. The Refinery worked so fast that it took me several months to realize that the work was completed. I was completely delivered from years of drug addiction.

Whichever way it works for you, whether quickly or slowly, **The Refinement Process** works!

Staging Area One

This is the first stop in The Refinery. Before entering the Reflection Station, you have to prepare yourself for the radical changes that you are about to undergo. You prepare yourself by getting an accurate view of your present state of being. Just like your dentist or surgeon requires x-ray or MRI images before they can correct the problem, you need an accurate picture of your life in order to correct your addiction problem.

Your self-images may be messy! You are the mess in the messy. At this stage, the "messed up" things in your life will *seem* messier! But, that's alright; it will all be worth it when you come out of The Refinery with the freedom that you desire. Therefore, it will be necessary for you to enter in to The Refinery with an honest assessment of who you are right now. Have great hope for your drug-free future!

In Staging Area One, prepare yourself to recognize your current realities. That means you must face the truth about the person you have become because of your addictions. It isn't a pretty picture, but, if you are honest with yourself, you already know that. **The Refinement Process** will not be pleasant, but you have to start at the beginning in order to get to the finish line.

In order to get the most out the upcoming Reflection Station, you must be honest and hopeful going in. The Reflection Station requires your honesty. Right now, you might not be a very honest person. You might be one who has lied and cheated your way through life in order to support your addictions. You might have burned all of your bridges. You might have burned all of the people who stood on those bridges ready to help and support you. Be honest about all of that. Own it!

The Reflection Station is most effective when you are hopeful. Perhaps it seems like all of your hope is gone. That simply is not true. Even though you may *feel* hopeless about your ability to be free from drug addictions, you probably have hope in other areas of your life. Maybe you hope for a better job, or you hope for somebody to love, or you hope for someone you love to be cured of a deadly disease. You see, all of your hope is not gone; you have hope in other areas of your life. Now, in The Refinery, you will learn how to transfer some of your hope over to your *desire* to be free from addictions.

There it is. In order to enter the Reflection Station, you need two things:

1. Honesty about who you are right now
2. Hope for your drug-free future

Do you have them? If you are ready, then let's get started.

The Reflection Station

Reflection: an image that is seen in a mirror or on a shiny surface, something that shows the effect, existence, or character of something else.

Part of every misery is, so to speak, the misery's shadow or reflection: the fact that you don't merely suffer but have to keep on thinking about the fact that you suffer. I not only live each endless day in grief, but live each day thinking about living each day in grief. C.S. Lewis

For now we see only a reflection as in a mirror; then we shall see face to face. Now I know in part; then I shall know fully, even as I am fully known. Paul [2]

My Story

After years and years of hopeless drug addiction, I came to a defining moment in my life. It happened one morning after a particularly hard night of drugging. In the bathroom, as I was brushing my teeth, I noticed the man in my mirror. I mean, for the first time in years, I really noticed him. His face was rail-thin, his eyes were sunken and they appeared dead. I literally did not recognize the person looking back at me! "Is that *me*? That can't be me!" The whole encounter deeply troubled me. I realized, for the first time in years, that I had lost my way. I was lost!

I believe that each person born in to this world has a predetermined purpose, plan, and path for his or her life. Many people never seek to understand their purpose in life. Instead, they choose to follow their own plan which puts them on a path ultimately leading to destruction. In order to arrive at your God-given destiny, you must seek to know your Purpose, understand The Plan for your life, and follow The Path. When people fail to seek their God-given Purpose, then they also fail to grasp their God-given Plan, therefore they consequently fail to recognize when they first stray from their God-given Path.

That is what happened to me. Because I ignored my purpose and plan, I strayed from my path. Gradually I crept farther and farther away from the pathway; step by step I wandered off the course which God chartered for my life. Sadly, for me, it was years later until I realized how far I had drifted.

"What do you want to be when you grow up, Ron?"

"I want to be an Architect!" was my enthusiastic reply.

I always loved to see how things worked. I loved to draw buildings, both floor plans and elevations. I loved to measure out and draw houses to scale: exterior columns, roof-lines, doorways, and windows. I was fascinated by how to make efficient use of space. My course was set; I was going to be an architect. But somewhere along the way I got sidetracked, and, because I stayed on the sidetrack, I did not notice when it sharply veered off course in a dangerous direction.

It is difficult to stay on course when you are high all the time. Drugs cause you to lose focus. They cause you to lose your direction and your drive. That is exactly what happened to me. What started off as a minor divergence caused me to end up a great distance from where I intended to be. I was lost. The tragic effect of being off-course was that not only had my direction changed, but I had also changed.

There I stood in front of my mirror, not recognizing where I was, and not recognizing who I was.

"What do you want to be when you grow up, Ron?

"A druggie?" my reflection replied.

Everything that we see is a shadow cast by that which we do not see.
Martin Luther King, Jr.

You are the Person in the Mirror

"What do you want to be when you grow up?"

Did anyone ask you that question when you were a kid? The list of youngsters' answers might include being a doctor, a lawyer, a teacher, a coach, a fireman, a policeman, and on and on. The one thing you never hear a kid say is, "I want to be a junkie when I grow up!"

The Search Begins Now

The Reflection Station is the next important phase in **The Refinement Process**. If you do not take this step then you can go no farther. This is the foundation of The Refinery. If you are serious about gaining your freedom from addictions, then you MUST take and complete this crucial step. If you are ready to become cleansed and whole, then let's get moving. Step out!

Let's take a couple of Action Steps that will help you to reflect on who you are, where you have been and where you are going.

Action Step 1

Find one of your childhood photos, preferably a snapshot or a school picture when you were five or six years old. Find one that was taken during your age of innocence. Now look at that face; really exam it. That was your face. Were you smiling? Did your eyes twinkle? That is the face of innocence and purity. Wouldn't it be great to return to a state of innocence? Wouldn't it be great to be pure once again? You may be thinking, *"That's impossible, look at me now. I'm a wreck. I'm too far gone."*

I say, NO! You are never too far gone. There is a way back to the innocence and purity of that young child. He or she is still alive in you. You owe it to that child in you, to return to a state of purity. It starts with reflection. Now, take your childhood picture and tape it to the corner of your bathroom mirror. Use it as a constant reminder of your journey back to innocence and purity.

Reflection, Your Starting Point for Refinement

There is a progression that starts with reflection and leads to refinement

Reflection leads to **Recognition**, if you are honest with yourself.

Recognition leads to **Realization**, if you are honest with yourself.

Realization leads to **Resignation**, if you sign-off on your old ways.

Resignation leads to **Refinement**, if you are tired of your impurities.

You look in the mirror to examine your face; now look at your life and examine the condition of your soul. Your life reflects your heart, your character. Have you ever taken a glance at your heart? That is called *soul searching*. It is amazing what you will find when you take the time to look.

Let's look at this progression. You already know that reflection is something that shows the effect, existence, or character of something else. When you reflect on something or someone you begin to recognize things about that object or person. Reflection leads to recognition.

Recognition is the act of knowing who or what someone or something is based upon previous knowledge or experience. Recognition is important because it helps you become familiar with the subject of the reflection. It is like when you run into someone that you have not seen in many years. At first, you may not know who the person is, but then he says or does something that causes you to recognize him. Recognition leads to realization.

Realization is the state of understanding or becoming aware of something. It could also be defined as the act of achieving something that was planned or hoped for. Let's continue with the example of the person whom you had not seen in many years. Once you recognize him, you may realize that you lent him money and he never repaid you. Further, you may realize a full repayment of the debt. First, you realized (became aware of) the person and the fact that he owed you money. Second, you realized (something that you hoped for) the repayment of the debt when he handed you the money owed.

Realization leads to resignation. Resignation is the feeling that something unpleasant is going to happen and cannot be changed. It's also the act of giving up a job or position in a formal or official way. The word resignation has the same root as the word signature, which means to endorse or write off something. Maybe, due to your drug addiction, you resigned yourself to the thought that you will always be an addict. Maybe you have signed off on your hopes for a better life without drugs.

Resignation is like a two-sided coin; each side has opposing viewpoints which lead to vastly different results. On one side, resignation can present a negative view of unpleasant, unchangeable things. If you are not careful, you might resign yourself to the thought *Things are so bad, why even bother to try to change?*

On the other side, resignation can present a positive view. Perhaps it could be the resigning from an old, unfulfilling lifestyle with the thought, *I'm signing off on my bondage to drugs!* One resignation tends toward signing off into destruction and defeat; the other resignation tends toward signing-up to begin positive lifestyle changes.

The latter type of resignation leads to refinement. Refinement should be the desired results you seek. When you resign yourself to refinement, you will begin to see better results. Now you can sign off from drug addiction and sign up for purity and the freedom from drug addiction.

Let's Face it

When I looked in the mirror, those many years ago, I saw the face of death staring back at me. I didn't recognize my face in the mirror. But, that was just the beginning of my transformation from death to life.

As water reflects the face, so one's life reflects the heart. Solomon [3]

One day, you too will face the person in your mirror. You don't know the hour or the day that it will happen for you. Maybe you are not ready for your date with the person in the mirror. I do know that when you are ready to truly face the person in the mirror, you will be ready for your transformation. When you are ready, that face in your mirror will plead with you for help. It will be your date with a brighter future, your future of freedom! But, first you have to face it.

Face the Facts: stop putting on a mask; what are you trying to hide?

Face the Fears: stop lying to yourself; you can be free.

Face the Folly: stop the foolishness.

Search me, O God, and know my heart: test me and know my anxious thoughts: See if there is any offensive way in me, and lead me in the way everlasting. David [4]

Generally, before you go out in public, you probably look in the mirror. Just a quick glance reveals anything about your appearance which might be out of order like hair not combed, facial blemishes, teeth not brushed, clothing mismatched, blouse unbuttoned, or slacks unzipped. Isn't it better to catch a view of that before you go out in public?

Then, after some adjustments, the mirror shows that you look great. People judge you by your outward appearance. And, although it is important to keep up appearances, you must be mindful of your inward appearance, too. It has been said that the eyes are the *windows of the soul*. When you look into the mirror, look into your eyes. Do you recognize the person in the reflection? How do you reflect on the inner you? Let's take a look.

Action Step 2

Use the following questions as an inner mirror, a mirror for your soul. As you reflect on your answers, know that there may be another perspective, another point of view you do not see. Be honest with yourself as you gaze into this *soul* mirror.

As you search yourself, look for scars. Reflect on the wounds which were self-inflicted as well as those inflicted by other people. Look for things that are obvious. Look for things that are hidden deep inside. Take time now to search yourself and find some answers. Be sure to write down your answers. You will need these written answers later.

> Ask yourself:
> > Who am I?
> > Why am I alive?
> > How did I get my life into this condition?
> > What will be my future?

NOTE: If you did not answer the previous questions, then do not continue. If you did not complete this Action Step then you are not ready to go on this journey. There are no shortcuts. It requires that you take first things first. Please, go back. Take the time to reflect and truthfully answer the questions. This work is the starting point for **The Refinement Process**. Believe me, it will be worth your investment of time and effort. Write down your answers.

In order to see where you are going, you have to know where you are. Even when you use a GPS to get the directions to your destination, it starts by determining your current location. The refiner starts by assaying the gold or silver ore to determine the current condition and the possible value of the finished metal.

Have you ever seen an infomercial for a new diet or an exercise program? To support their claims of fabulous results, the sponsors always show the BEFORE and AFTER photos. The after photo always looks much better than the before photo. There has to be a way to see the results; otherwise, why buy their program? People want to see results.

In The Refinery, you want to see results. So, let's take a BEFORE and AFTER snapshot.

Ask yourself two questions (be sure to write down your answers):

1. What was my life like before I started using drugs?

Only you can answer what your life was like before the entrance of drugs. Were you contented or confused? Were you satisfied or dissatisfied? Were you happy or miserable? It is important to identify your pre-addiction state of being. Many people choose drugs as a way to self-medicate their hurtful, miserable, or unsatisfactory conditions.

2. What can my life be like after drugs are gone?

Imagine all of the wonderful changes. Consider all of the possibilities for your life once you are freed from the chains that prevent you from realizing your full potential. Consider a healthier body or a wealthier life, when all your money is not being wasted on addictions. Consider restored relationships with your family. Consider new relationships with exciting new friends.

When you have completed writing your answers, set them aside. We will take a look at them later in The Refinery.

In reflecting, it is sometimes helpful when another person holds up the mirror. This is called intervention, when family or friends help you to see some of your flaws, with the hope that you will recognize them, admit them, and get help resolving them. Here, again, you have the flow from Reflection to Recognition to Resignation to Refinement.

Now, let's take a look at a man who was brought face to face with the man in the mirror.

Refinement Hero

King David, the ruler of ancient Israel, had a position of power and prestige. As king, he could command anything that his heart desired. He had authority over life and death. In those days, it was common for kings to have many wives and concubines (girlfriends). King David was no exception. He had seven wives and many concubines. With all of that, he was still not satisfied.

The story goes… One night, when King David walked on the roof of his palace, he saw a beautiful young woman bathing in her nearby house. He asked his counselors about her and they said that she was the wife of one of his soldiers. He gave orders to have her brought to him. He took advantage and slept with her. Later, she sent word to the king that she was pregnant.

Upon receiving this news, King David set in motion a devious plan to cover up his sin. First, he brought the woman's husband home from the battlefield for a little rest and recuperation. He hoped that the weary soldier would sleep with his wife, therein making it look like she had been impregnated by her husband. However, out of loyalty to the king and to his fellow-soldiers, the man refused to go home to his wife.

Having failed with that ruse, King David went to Plan B. He sent the soldier back to the battlefield with sealed orders for the General to place the soldier at the frontline of the war. The soldier fought gallantly and died in battle. This left the soldier's wife, a grieving widow, available to King David to marry, thus hiding the sexual indiscretion, and making it appear that the pregnancy was legitimate. Indeed, King David married his soldier's widow and it appeared that his sin was hidden.

But King David was about to discover the man in the mirror. The Lord sent the Prophet Nathan to hold up a mirror before the king. He did so by telling this story to the king. Nathan said,

"There were two men in a certain town, one rich and the other poor. The rich man had a very large number of sheep and cattle, but the poor man had nothing except one little ewe lamb he had bought. He raised it, and it grew up with him and his children. It shared his food, drank from his cup and even slept in his arms. It was like a daughter to him.

"Now a traveler came to the rich man, but the rich man refrained from taking one of his own sheep or cattle to prepare a meal for the traveler who had come to him. Instead, he took the ewe lamb that belonged to the poor man and prepared it for the one who had come to him."

Upon hearing this story King David was furious. He was so angry that he pronounced a judgment against the rich man. He said,

"As surely as the LORD lives, the man who did this must die! He must pay for that lamb four times over, because he did such a thing and had no pity"

Then Nathan said to David, *"You are the man!"* [5]

Imagine David's shock when he recognized his guilty face in the "mirror." I imagine that he was horrified by his own hideous reflection. There he was, a rich powerful man, too self-absorbed to see how his own lust, fraud, deception, and murder had destroyed a family.

Maybe your own lust and deceptions have destroyed your friendships and family. Maybe your own greed and theft have left you embarrassed, shameful, and guilty. Believe me, I know those feelings. I have been there and done that! Well, what are you going to do about it? Now is neither the time nor the place for self-pity. Now is the time for you to take action.

This Reflection Station can be one of the most intense phases of The Refinery. If you have been sincere up to this point, you have experienced some intense emotions. That's alright; this is going to hurt some, like cutting out the infection in a wound so it can properly heal. You might feel sadness, confusion, remorse, anger, shame, helplessness; what a mess! Trust me, in time, you will feel better.

Are you ready for your next station? If so, please continue on.

Reflection Review Platform

In your reflection, you need to identify two key characteristics:

1. Hope for your drug-free future
2. Honesty about who you are right now

There is a natural and spiritual progression from Reflection to Refinement:

Reflection leads to Recognition
Recognition leads to Realization
Realization leads to Resignation
Resignation leads to Refinement

Reflection helps you to:

Face the Facts
Face the Fears
Face the Folly

Staging Area Two

You have just completed the Reflection Station. I told you, things might get messy! Was I right? Whenever past and present failures are dredged up there is a stench. Do not be afraid to face your failures. Do not be afraid to smell the rotten odor of your life. It is necessary to see and smell how bad it is in order to know how great it can be.

The important thing is that you made it this far. You survived. And now your messy life is being staged to be cleansed and purified. In the refinement of gold, the ore is melted and the impurities rise to the top. There they are identified and removed.

The next stop in The Refinery is the Repentance Station. But first, let's get you staged and ready to enter this critical phase of **The Refinement Process**.

In this Staging Area, take time now to examine the road that you are on. Look at where you are today and find some answers. When you consider your current state, ask yourself:

> Am I where I want to be in my life? If not, ask yourself: Where do I want to be?
> How much longer can I go on this way?
> What keeps me from getting back on the right track?
> Where will I end up if I keep going this way?
> Am I really ready for a positive change in my life?

Two things are required of you in the Repentance Station:

1. Sincerity (no deceit, hypocrisy, or falseness). Be honest. Be earnest.

2. Submission (yield and surrender). Stop resisting.

NOTE: If you are not ready for a positive change in your life, then you are not ready to proceed. That is alright. Just know that there is help and hope here in The Refinery. Come back when your life cannot get any worse.

If you *are* ready for a positive change, then let's proceed.

The Repentance Station

Repentance: deep sorrow, compunction, or contrition for a past sin, wrongdoing, or the like; regret for a past action.

Then David said to Nathan, *"I have sinned against the LORD."* [6]

If you remember from the Reflection Station, King David saw his horrible image in the "mirror". His reaction is the key to the next station in **The Refinement Process**.

When you repent, you admit your faults and ask for forgiveness. David understood that if he were totally honest with himself, then he had to confess his evil acts and repent. His repentance caused a firestorm of events to occur in his life. The first arose with the death of David's infant son, and later continued with a series of hurtful family matters. But, the Refiner was at work and David's life became His Masterpiece. You will find out more about the Refiner as you move through this station.

Standing at the Crossroads

You made it through the Reflection Station and now you have arrived here at the Repentance Station. Having made it this far, you now are at a decision point in The Refinery; you are standing at a crossroads. There is the road that continues the way you have been going, (drug abuse, heartache, shame, and loss of family and friends). That road is a dead-end leading to the destruction of your life and premature death. But, there is a road that crosses that road, a different road that leads you to an addiction-free life. You are at that place of decision, the crossroads.

There is a way that seems right to a man, But its end is the way of death. Solomon [7]

For many people, the hardest words to say are, *I was wrong* and *I am sorry*. You may not like to admit failure or defeat. You may not like to admit that your actions caused damage or injury to someone else. Usually, that is because of your own foolish pride. You want to appear that you have everything under control, when in reality, something has you under its control. Drugs are considered controlled substances, but, they are also controlling substances. When you are on drugs your life is out of your control.

Repentance occurs when you admit your current state of being. You admit you have made a mess of your life. You admit you are unable to stop your downward freefall. Be big enough to admit your addictions and look for help in overcoming them. Help is here in the Repentance Station. Let's get started!

Repentance occurs when you admit that you need help. Admit that your feeble *will power* is no match for your addictions. Since you are powerless to change, you need a power that is greater than you. How do I know? I used to always say, "I can quit using drugs anytime I choose to quit." That was my boastful pride talking. In reality, I had tried numerous times to quit and each time I had failed. My will power was really *won't power!* I told myself, "I won't do that again. I mean it, this time I won't get high!" That all sounded good, but then I would go and get high. So much for will power. Does that sound familiar? Have you been there and done that? Are you there right now? If so, don't fret. There is a power that far surpasses your power.

The subtitle of The Refinery states, **Overcoming Drug Addictions Through The Supernatural Power Available to You.** Allow me to introduce to you the power at work in The Refinery. He is the Chief Operations Officer. I call Him…

The Refiner

When I was a child, I knew Him as the God of my loving parents, Benjamin and Elsie Gibson. Unfortunately, I was limited in my desire to know Him for myself. Perhaps the Apostle Paul described my plight when he wrote,

When I was a child, I spoke as a child, I understood as a child, I thought as a child... [8]

I grew up with a purely religious, impersonal view of Jesus. I saw statues of Him on the cross and I thought, *poor guy, it's too bad that you ended up that way*. Mine was an immature understanding of the Lord.

Throughout the Scripture, Jesus was referred to in many different ways. He was described as the Good Shepherd, the Captain of the Host (army), the Son of Man, the Son of God, the Fisher of Men, the Sower, the Teacher, the Healer, and much more.

Paul went on to state,

...but when I became a man, I put away childish things. [9]

When I finally grew up, I came to know this Jesus for myself. Please allow me to introduce you to Him, **Jesus, the Refiner**.

Not Religion, It's About Relationship

Most religions are mankind's attempts to reach God. People create systems, doctrines, rules and regulations; they create sacred ceremonies and traditions, all in an attempt to connect with God.

Jesus never came to create a religion. In fact, you can see where He quickly halted any attempt to establish a religious order. It happened when Jesus went up a high mountain to be alone with three of his disciples, Peter, James, and John. Suddenly, before their eyes, Jesus was transformed (metamorphosed). In Sci-Fi terms, He morphed or shape-shifted. His body and clothing glowed intensely and He was surrounded by an extremely bright light. His disciples also saw Elijah and Moses talking with him.

The disciples witnessed this great scene: Moses, who represented God's Law; Elijah, who represented God's Prophets; and Jesus, who represented the reuniting of mankind to God. They were astonished. Not knowing what to do, Peter said, *"Master, it is good for us to be here: and let us make three tabernacles; one for You, and one for Moses, and one for Elias."* [10] Basically, Peter's idea for the tabernacles was to establish a religion.

Jesus did not even acknowledge Peter's remarks. Instead, out of the heavy clouds which shrouded the mountain, the voice of God declared, **"This is my beloved Son, Hear Him."** [11] Then suddenly, Moses and Elijah were gone. Jesus turned to his disciples and simply instructed them to tell nobody what they saw until after the Son of Man is resurrected from the dead.

If Jesus had wanted to establish a religion, the Mountain of His Transfiguration would have been the perfect place. Think of it, the Tabernacle of Moses on the right, the Tabernacle of Elijah on the left and the grandest of all, center stage, the Tabernacle of Jesus. But, His intent was not to do His own will; He came to fulfill the will of his Heavenly Father.

Jesus had previously announced His plans:

The Spirit of the Lord is upon me, because he hath anointed me to preach the gospel to the poor; he hath sent me to heal the brokenhearted, to preach deliverance to the captives, and recovering of sight to the blind, to set at liberty them that are bruised, to preach the acceptable year of the Lord. [12]

He did not come to establish religion. He came to reestablish mankind's relationship with God.

Not religion (mankind's attempt to reach God), but instead *relationship* (God's desire to have a royal family). Jesus came for the poor, the brokenhearted, the captives, the blind, and those who are bruised. His only message for you is that the Kingdom of God has come for your benefit.

For God so loved the world, that he gave his only begotten Son, that whosoever believeth in him should not perish, but have everlasting life. For God sent not his Son into the world to condemn the world; but that the world through him might be saved. [13]

> **Jesus came for the Refinement of mankind.**
> **He came to us as the Refiner.**

So now you recognize the Refiner. You may not know Him, but you are coming to know who He is. The Refiner of your soul is Jesus, the Christ! He is the only one who has the power and the willingness to rescue and refine you. There is none other.

This may not be what you want to hear, but you need to hear it and accept it. See what the Refiner has to say to you,

And blessed is he, whosoever shall not be offended in me. [14]

Notice that He said **whosoever**. That means you! He said blessed is he who is not offended because of Him. You have the choice now to continue with **The Refinement Process** fully recognizing that the Refiner is Jesus Christ.

I realize that some of you will be offended by the mention of His name. If that is you, I simply ask,

Is your offense of Jesus greater than your desire to be free from drug addictions?

Think about it. What means more to you, your offense over Jesus being the Refiner or continuing to be dragged to your destruction by addictions which have control over you? The Refiner states the person who is not offended in Him *is blessed*. So, if that is true then the opposite is also true; the person who *is* offended in Him is cursed!

What the Refiner is asking of you is such a small thing, especially compared to what He is doing for you and what He is doing inside of you. He is cleansing you; He is purifying you; He is forgiving you. He is releasing you from drug addictions.

Jesus, the Refiner, was perfect in every way. He never sinned neither did He do any wrong.

God made him who had no sin to be sin for us, so that in him we might become the righteousness of God. [15]

Jesus lived a perfect, sin-free life; therefore, He was the perfect sacrifice so that we could have atonement for our sins. He was crucified. He died nailed to a wooden cross. He was buried in a tomb. But, on the third day, He was empowered to rise from the dead.

The Refiner has unlimited power. He is making it available for you right now. But, in order for Him to use that power to refine you, you have to admit that you are powerless to change yourself. That's what **The Refinement Process** is all about. Repent and admit that you need the Refiner's powerful help. When you accept His help, He will use His supernatural power to raise you up from your deadly addictions. Accept Him as the Refiner.

The first condition is repentance, which means a change of mind. Formerly I thought sin a pleasant thing, but now I have changed my mind about it; formerly I thought the world an attractive place, but now I know better; formerly I regarded it a miserable business to be a Christian, but now I think differently. Once I thought certain things delightful, now I think them vile; once I thought other things utterly worthless, now I think them most precious. That is a change of mind, and that is repentance. Watchman Nee

Change Your Mind; Change Your Life

Philip Seymour Hoffman, Heath Ledger, Whitney Houston, Amy Winehouse, and the King of Pop, Michael Jackson, these are just a handful of the many famous people who recently died of drug overdoses. They each had remarkable talent, wealth and fame. Probably, they all had more movies, songs, and performances to contribute to our lives and culture. Their stories might help you to reconsider the path for your own life. Let's take an Action Step.

Action Step

Make your own list of celebrities whose untimely deaths were the results of drug or alcohol addiction (or drug/alcohol related).

1. Do an internet search of "celebrity deaths by overdose."
2. Make a list of ten stars that died in the past ten years.
3. Pick two from your list with whom you closely identify; have a photo of each person.
4. Now do an internet search the life stories of both celebrities.
5. Read each celebrity's life story and write down the things that are similar to your life story: broken family, abandonment, divorce, early death of a loved one, poor choice of friends, any kind of physical, emotional or sexual abuse, any mental health issues, negative attitudes or destructive behaviors.
6. Write down how the celebrities each coped with their troubles.
7. Now write down how you are coping with your own troubles.

Did you find some similarities with the celebrity's journey and your journey? Are you trying to cope with your addictions in the same way they coped with theirs? A wise person learns from the mistakes of other people and adjusts his own actions thereby avoiding a similar tragic destiny.

Do not conform to the pattern of this world, but be transformed by the renewing of your mind. Paul [16]

For the many years I was addicted to drugs, I was not satisfied with my life. I realized there was more to life than getting high. Deep down I always knew my lifestyle was wrong. I had not been raised to use drugs. I came from a good home with loving and supportive parents.

Drugging was my way of rebelling against all authority. I was always an outsider, therefore, drugging was my way of fitting in with the other "freaks"; it was my way of coping with other major issues in my life. Actually, it was my way of running away and avoiding the hurtful things in my life. Can you relate? Drugging was my way out....far out!

We all want progress, but if you're on the wrong road, progress means doing an about-turn and walking back to the right road; in that case, the man who turns back soonest is the most progressive. C.S. Lewis

You Need a Course Correction

We have all, at one time, found ourselves going down the road heading in the wrong direction.

Drug addiction is that road which leads to a dead end. It is time for you to turn around. It is time for you to change your course. Get on the right road; it leads to a great new life. The Refiner said,

"I am the way, the truth, and the life..." John 14:6

Get on the right road, going the right way. Ignorance occurs when you turn your back on the truth. By ignoring the truth you set yourself up to be deceived. When you turn your back to the Refiner, you are heading in the wrong way.

When you turn *toward* the Refiner, you turn your back on the past hurts, the past troubles, the past disappointments. You can then face the solution for your messed up life. The Refiner IS the solution to your problems. He IS the supernatural power you need to overcome your addictions. He can rescue you, if you let Him.

Now, let's look at a man who faced a crossroads moment of decision. He stood at the door to the Repentance Station. His name was Saul.

Refinement Hero

Saul was not addicted to drug, however, he was addicted to his religion. He was a zealot who was so absorbed in his religion that he became an extreme terrorist. Anyone who didn't follow Saul's religion was subject to his harsh tactics. This is how he was described:

But Saul began to destroy the church. Going from house to house, he dragged off both men and women and put them in prison. Acts 8:3 (NIV)

Meanwhile, Saul was still breathing out murderous threats against the Lord's disciples. He went to the high priest and asked him for letters to the synagogues in Damascus, so that if he found any there who belonged to the Way, whether men or women, he might take them as prisoners to Jerusalem. Acts 9:1-2 (NIV)

Saul, on his way to Damascus, had a close encounter with the Refiner. Suddenly, as he approached the city, a blinding light shone all around him. It was so powerful that he was thrown to the ground and he heard a voice saying, *"Saul, Saul, why are you troubling me?"* It was the Refiner calling his name and asking him to give an account of his reckless actions!

Saul asks, *"Who are you, Lord?"*

The Lord said, *"I am Jesus, whom you are troubling. Why are you fighting this useless battle against me?"*

Saul, trembling, asked, *"Lord, what do You want me to do?"*

In this story, found in Acts 9:3-8, we see an incredible encounter between the Refiner and Saul. Saul, like many people, was heading in the wrong direction. And yet, he found his way to the Repentance Station.

That was the point where Saul began to experience positive change in his life. He quickly recognized that he was in opposition to the Refiner. His response is the key to the Repentance Station. With that one question, **"Lord, what do You want me to do?"**, Saul was placed on a new course. His life was changed forever! Not only was his life changed, but the Refiner even gave him a new name, Paul. He became the Refiner's masterpiece of faith and courage.

My Story

Drug addiction had robbed me of all my youthful ambition. It had stolen my dreams of a successful life. My addictions had control of me. It was the first thing on my mind when I awoke and it was the last thing on my mind when I crashed at night. *How will I get high today?* It had become the overriding motivation of my pitiful life.

As I continued my downward spiral, I kept thinking that there had to be a better life for me. All the while I kept thinking of the statement my friend Marva had made:

"You can be with your drugs or you can be with me, but you can't have us both. You decide!"

After several days of some deep soul searching I made my decision. I chose Marva. She was different from my other friends. She was so alive and free. I, on the other hand, was being destroyed day by day. For me, it was time for positive change to begin.

As I nervously dialed her phone number, my mind raced with thoughts of what I would say.

"Hi, Marva, this is Ron. How are you?"

"Oh, Hi, Ron, I've been thinking about you. How are you?"

"I'm okay. I wanted to talk with you about a decision I made. I reflected on what you said. You gave me a really clear choice; I could be with the drugs or I could be with you, but I couldn't be with both."

"And what did you decide?" she asked.

"Marva, I want to be with you. Meeting you was the best thing that has happened to me in a long time." I confided.

"Is that so?" she said with some hesitation.

"Yeah, that's right. Listen, in July, I am going to leave Boston and relocate to Rochester. And when I come there I will be drug-free!"

She paused and simply said, "Okay, we will see."

We said our goodbyes and ended the phone call. Now, I was on the spot! I just told this woman I was going to be drug-free when I moved there in a few months. What was I going to do? I didn't know how to get free from the drugs. At that point of my life, I really didn't know the Refiner and His supernatural power to rescue me. This was my simple plea:

"Lord, I've really made a mess of myself and my life. I want to be free from this addiction to drugs, but I can't do this myself; I tried and I failed. But, I know that you can do it! If I let you, will you take these drugs out of my life? I surrender to you; please take them from me."

I, like Saul, admitted that I was wrong and the Refiner began His work on me.

> **The ore cannot refine itself;**
>
> **it takes the Refiner to purify it.**

What You Must Do to be Refined

When you come to the place where you admit that you cannot change yourself, then you are ready for the Refiner to work on you.

If you are not ready to repent, no one can convince or persuade you. If you are not ready, here is a good place to bail out, but I sincerely hope that you don't bail. The Refiner is patiently waiting for you to complete this Repentance Station. So, I caution you; do not wait too long. The longer you wait the greater the toll your addiction will have on you until there is nothing left. Now is the time for you to repent. There is no better time than right now.

At this point in the Repentance Station, your question to me might be, "What must I do to be rescued, refined and purified?" Let's look at how the Refiner answers that question.

Very truly I tell you, no one can see the kingdom of God unless they are born again. John 3:3 (NIV)

He went on to explain the purpose and promises of refinement,

For God so loved the world that he gave his one and only Son, that whoever believes in him shall not perish but have eternal life. For God did not send his Son into the world to condemn the world, but to save the world through him. John 3:16-17 (NIV)

The key to the Repentance Station can be found in Paul's letter to the people of Rome.

If you declare with your mouth, "Jesus is Lord," and believe in your heart that God raised him from the dead, you will be saved. For it is with your heart that you believe and are justified, and it is with your mouth that you profess your faith and are saved. As Scripture says, "Anyone who believes in him will never be put to shame." Romans 10:9-11 (NIV)

Once you submit yourself to the Refiner's hand then you are ready for the next station in **The Refinement Process**.

The Refiner

He sat by the fire of seven-fold heat,
As He watched by the precious ore.
And closer He bent with a searching gaze
As He heated it more and more.

He knew He had ore that could stand the test
And He wanted the finest gold,
To mold as a crown for the King to wear,
Set with gems of price untold.

So He laid our gold in the burning fire,
Though we fain would have said Him, "Nay."
And He watched the dross that we had not seen,
As it melted and passed away.

And the gold grew brighter, and yet more bright
And our eyes were so dim with tears.
As we saw the fire, not the Master's hand,
And questioned with anxious fear.

Yet our gold shone out with a richer glow,
As it mirrored a Form above
That bent o'er the fire, though unseen by us
With a look of infinite love.

Can we think that it pleases His loving heart
To cause a moment of pain?
Ah, no, but He saw through the present cross
The bliss of eternal gain.

So He waited there with a watchful eye,
With a love that is strong and sure,
And His gold did not suffer a bit more heat
Than was needed to make it pure!
  Source Unknown

Repentance Review Platform

Repentance occurs when you admit your current state of being.
Repentance occurs when you admit that you need help.

Refinement requires the Refiner:

The ore cannot refine itself; it takes the Refiner to purify it.

The Refiner of your soul is Jesus the Christ.

He wants to establish a relationship with you; *not* religion.

Are you offended by Jesus?

Is your offense of Jesus greater than your desire to be free from drug addictions?

When you come to the place where you admit that you cannot change yourself, then you are ready for the Refiner to go to work on you.

The Refiner IS the power to overcome any addiction.
The Refiner IS the solution to your problems. He can rescue you, if you let Him.

Ask the Refiner to forgive you. He is willing.
Ask Him to cleanse and purify you. He is able.

STAGING AREA THREE

This Staging Area is to prepare you for the Redemption Station. This is where the Refiner will begin to cleanse and purify you. He is recreating you as His masterpiece. Let's pause here a moment and make absolutely sure that you realize what is happening to your life.

At the Reflection Station, you came to know that you are in rough shape. You are like raw metal ore. There is value in the rock, but not until all the impurities are eliminated. The Refiner sees value in you; but in order for you to live a successful life, the impurities must be removed.

You have just passed through the Repentance Station. Presently, some of the biggest impurities in your life are your addictions. Hopefully, by now, you have admitted it and asked for the Refiner's help to rescue and refine you. Cry out from the bottom of your heart:

Lord Jesus, my Refiner, I know that I am a sinner, and I am sorry for my sin. I repent of it and I turn to You by faith right now. I believe that You are the Son of God. Thank You for dying on the cross for me and paying the price for my sins. I ask You to come into my life now and be my Rescuer and my Refiner. I surrender myself to You. Refine me and help me to live my life for You. Thank You, Lord. In Jesus name I pray. Amen.

Congratulations! Welcome to the Refiner's family! You just made the best decision you will ever make. Get ready, my friend, for the biggest, best change of your life. You are staged to go from impurity to purity, from imperfection to perfection. When purity of spirit comes, then that which is impure passes away. When perfection of spirit comes, then that which is imperfect passes away. Purity and perfection of spirit, through the Refiner, always trumps impurity and imperfection!

You have already done some of the hard stuff, but your power is limited. But, there is a Supernatural power available to you. From here on the Refiner will do most of the heavy lifting, His power is limitless.

Let's proceed!

The Redemption Station

Redemption: the act of making something better or more acceptable; the act of exchanging something for money; an award, etc.

For you were bought at a price; therefore glorify God in your body and in your spirit, which are God's. 1 Corinthians 6:20 (NKJV)

Welcome! You have arrived at the Redemption Station. This is the most exciting and remarkable station in **The Refinement Process**. Up to now, you were in control of things. You had to reflect; you recognized your helpless and hopeless condition. You had to Repent; you admitted that you could not change yourself and you needed the Refiner's powerful help. You made it through those stations. From here on, the Refiner takes over. Your part is to trust, believe, and obey His directions. Now it is time for the Refiner to begin His work on you.

Kidnapped and Held For Ransom

Because of sin, all of mankind was abducted by an enemy, Satan. He kidnapped us from the real life, that life which God had planned for you and me. We were held hostage until our ransom was paid. As you saw, there was only one person qualified to pay our ransom. That person is the Refiner, Jesus.

The Redemption Station is where you acknowledge and accept that your ransom is paid. Through His death (on the cross), His burial (three days in the grave) and His resurrection, He defeated Satan. The Refiner made payment for your release; release from the addictions.

The Refiner paid it in full with His life. He gave His life a ransom for many.

The moment you repented, the Refiner released you from your debt. He gave His life as a ransom for you and me. Your debt was paid and you are free!

Free Delivery, Paid In Full

At this point, you will need some basic background in order to understand the magnificent work that is occurring in you, and the work truly is magnificent! There are some basic truths that will help you appreciate your total deliverance from drug addictions.

> **Redemption is deliverance as a result of the payment of a price.**

When I think of the term deliverance, I think of movement from one place to another. Mail is delivered from the sender's location to the recipient's address. Freight is shipped from a warehouse and delivered to a factory or store. Products are delivered from an online retailer to your home.

Often I use the phrase *deliverance from drugs* or *deliverance from addictions*. By that I don't mean that a person moves from one location to another. I simply mean that the addiction goes away; it leaves. When you give your letters or packages to the postal worker, that person takes them away to be delivered to the addressee. That mail is picked up and delivered from you to another place. Through the supernatural power of the Refiner, which is available to you, drugs and addictions can be picked up and taken away and delivered back to hell (where they came from and where they belong).

Many times, when you see an advertisement on television or on the internet, the seller will offer free shipping and handling, or free delivery. That is an added incentive to buy their product. In truth, there is no free delivery; it simply does not exist. Somebody always pays. And that somebody is you! The seller simply calculated his shipping costs into the price that is charged to you. It appears that you aren't paying extra delivery charges, but you are.

In contrast, when the Refiner delivers you from drug addictions, there is no additional cost to you. That's right, you pay no extra delivery charges. But, remember, there is no free delivery. In the case of your deliverance, somebody paid the price. That somebody was Christ, the Redeemer. The delivery charges were included in the redemption package, paid in full by the Refiner for you. You receive it free, but it cost Him everything! He gave His all so that you could go free.

Redemption is rescue from the grip of addictions, and much, much more. Through your drug addictions and other destructive acts, you incurred a sin debt to God. It is a debt that you can never repay. Jesus the Refiner paid a debt; your debt that He did not owe. How and why did He pay the price to free you?

How did He pay it? - He paid your debt with His own blood. He was beaten, tortured and executed for you. The magnitude of our sin was so great that it required His perfect sacrifice in order to pay it off.

In fact, according to the Law of Moses, nearly everything was purified with blood. For without the shedding of blood, there is no forgiveness. Hebrews 9:22 (NLT)

Because Jesus the Refiner, lived a perfect life, free from sin, His sacrificial death was not for His own sin, but it was for ours - yours, mine and the sins of all the peoples of the world.

In him we have redemption through his blood, the forgiveness of sins, in accordance with the riches of God's grace that he lavished on us. With all wisdom and understanding. Ephesians 1:7-8 (NIV)

Why did He pay it? - The Refiner did it because of His awesome love for you. He loves you more than you love yourself. He did it so that you can live a successful life, free from drug addictions. He has already done the hard part. Now, can you sense Him working on your heart and your head? He is cleansing you from the inside out. The Refiner told us:

…I am come that they might have life, and that they might have it more abundantly. John 10:10b

> **God loved you first. God loved you best. God loved you completely**

And, it is not because we deserved it. In fact, we did not deserve anything that He did for us. There is nothing that we can do to deserve His great love. We simply receive it, accept it and give Him thanks for it. God recognized that we were unable to free ourselves, therefore He sent a Redeemer.

No creature that deserved Redemption would need to be redeemed. They that are whole need not the physician. Christ died for men precisely because men are not worth dying for; to make them worth it. C.S. Lewis

What Does He See When He Looks At Me

Often, there is a stark contrast between what you see in yourself and what the Refiner sees when He looks at you. You see your impurities and imperfections; the Refiner sees you purified and perfected. You see past failures; He sees your potential for greatness! Let's look at this as you take another Action Step forward.

Action Step 1

Go back to the Action Step 2 in the Reflection Station. There you wrote your answers to four important questions. Through your answers you gave a self-assessment of the who, the what, and the why of your life. Remember, the Refiner also has an opinion of you. It is found in the Scriptures. See how He answers those same questions concerning you. Now, let's compare your point of view with the Refiner's point of view:

1. What does the Refiner say about who I am?

He said you were created in His image and likeness… Genesis 1:26

He said you are fearfully and wonderfully made! Psalms 139:14

2. What does the Refiner say about why am I alive?

He said you are *created for His pleasure*… Psalms 149:4

He said you are to be fruitful, multiply, replenish the world, subdue it and have dominion over His creation. Genesis 1:28

3. What does the Refiner say about how I got in my present condition?

He said there is a path before each person that seems right, but it ends in death. Proverbs 14:12 (NLT)

4. What does the Refiner say about what will be my future?

He said *you shall reign with Him forever*… Revelation 22:5 (NKJV)

How do your answers compare with the Refiner's answers? Your answers may reflect helplessness or hopelessness. His answers reflect His helpfulness towards you and His hope for you to have a better future.

Take a look at how this played out in my life.

My Story

As a kid I attended a small local church in my hometown Canandaigua, New York. I was a member of the Youth Group and I was very active in Sunday school. I knew about Jesus, and I really thought that I knew Him, but as I entered my mid-teen years, I started to drift from the "church-kids" over to the "cool-kids".

Sure, I continued to go to church, but that was basically because my Dad and Mom made me. Christianity was my parents' religion. My religion was *The Church of If It Feels Good Do It*. And boy was I doing it. I was doing it to death! The problem was, MY religion was leading me straight to my grave.

Fast-forward many years later; there I was, pleading in desperation and crying out:

"Lord, I've really made a mess of myself and my life. I want to be free from this addiction to drugs, but I can't do this myself; I tried and I failed. But, I know that you can do it! If I let you, will you take these drugs out of my life? I surrender to you; please take them from me."

That was the first time in many years I prayed for God to help me. I hadn't been inside a church in almost ten years. How absurd of me to think that the Lord would help me. But, that is just what He did. He started with my heart and then He worked on my head.

Remember, I had told my girlfriend Marva, I was relocating to Rochester, NY, to be closer to her, and that when I got there I would be drug-free. Well, I had made my bold statement to her in the month of May and my plan was to move right after the Fourth of July holiday. But, as the date to move grew closer, I started to have some second thoughts about successfully kicking my addictions. I didn't have second thoughts about wanting to quit using drugs; my second thoughts were about *could I really succeed?*

As the Independence Day holiday weekend approached, my mind was so screwed up that my prevailing thought was, *Since I will no longer be using drugs, I might as well go out in a blaze of glory!* By blaze of glory I meant, *I'm going to get totally wasted and do any and all the drugs that I can get my hands on!*

And sadly, that is exactly what I did. My friends were sorry to know I was leaving them for greener pastures; so the Fourth of July was my going away party. And boy did I get lit up! I smoked some weed, I snorted some coke, and I dropped some Quaaludes. I drank lots of alcohol and ingested whatever else was handed to me.

And even though I was *lit up*, the Refiner was at work, lighting up The Refinery fire. My head was so messed up that He started by grabbing my heart. Wow, did He ever grab it!

I awoke the next morning with a drug and alcohol hang-over, but something was different.

Obviously, that was not my first drug hang-over. They were fairly common; however, on that July morning, just hours before I was to move to Rochester, I felt something I had not felt in years. I felt remorse! I mean, big time REMORSE! I actually felt ashamed of myself. I was so loaded down with guilt and shame that, by comparison, it made the hang-over seem like a mild affliction.

Without me knowing it, the Refiner had turned up the flames. My heart was burning and not like the heartburn you get when you eat too much pizza. What I was experiencing was more like the heart burn of deep sorrow and agony because I knew I had failed Marva, I had failed myself, but most of all, I had failed God! He was at work on my heart, making sure I would never, and I mean never, forget my painful remorse.

With my heart still sizzling from the purifying flames of The Refinery, He went to work on my head. The fog of the drug hang-over started to burn off, and my thoughts became clear. More clear than they had been in years. It was like a shining light came on and I could start to make sense of it all. I realized what I needed to do. I had to make my peace with the Refiner because I began to see that He was first and foremost, my Redeemer.

Your Believer and Your Thinker

You see, the first time I pleaded with Him to take the drugs away, I told Him that I surrendered myself to Him. But, it was a lie! I had not surrendered to Him at all. My heart and my head were surrendered to the drugs. What now became clear to me was that I had to totally surrender to the Refiner so He could redeem me.

> ### Your Heart is your Believer,
> ### Your Head is your Thinker

The Refiner wants to start working on your heart; your Believer.

Trust in the LORD with all your heart *and lean not on your own understanding; in all your ways submit to him, and he will make your paths straight.* Proverbs 3:5-6 (NIV)

The work of the Redemption Station continues as you come to believe that the Refiner can rescue you. Do you believe it? For you, it may be a leap of faith, especially if you do not know the Refiner. It is hard to trust someone you do not know. It is hard, but not impossible. The Refiner makes it easy to trust Him. Think about it, if you are drowning and there is no way that you can keep yourself afloat; then the lifeguard reaches out and grabs you. Will you trust the lifeguard? You bet you will! The lifeguard is your only hope of survival.

The Refiner is the lifeguard. He is your only hope of survival. Trust Him with your whole heart. He is here to rescue you; He is here to save your life. He has already begun His work on your heart.

Now, He is also working on your head; your Thinker.

And do not be conformed to this world: but **be transformed by the renewing of your mind**, *that you may prove what is that good, and acceptable, and perfect, will of God.* Romans 12:2 (NKJV)

The classic description of insanity is to continue doing the same thing over and over thinking that you will get a different result. You have tried over and over to free yourself from the grip of addictions, but over and over you failed. That means that your way out of addictions is not working. Think about it. There has to be a different way to succeed. And there is. You are right in the midst of it, The Refinery. Let the Refiner do His work on you. He will change your way of thinking. He will give you the best results!

In my case, as soon as I prayed for help, He helped me. To me that is amazing! His help changed my way of thinking. I always thought drug rehabilitation required a lengthy process which included painful detox, months in a residential rehab center (with the latest methods of psycho-therapeutic behavioral modification), possible use of replacement prescription drugs, and a lifetime of sobriety support group meetings.

But the Refiner had a method far superior to all of those. His method included absolutely NO cravings, NO withdrawal pains or complications, NO rehab centers, NO behavior modification therapy, NO 12-Step programs, just total deliverance from my drug demons! Finally, the monkey was off my back. In fact, it was so quick, I did not fully realize He'd totally freed me from years of drug addictions. I was redeemed!

Of course, your results may vary. "Aha," you may think, "**The Refinement Process** doesn't work for everybody." You are correct.

Sadly, it will not work for everybody, BUT not because the process doesn't work; rather, because not everybody will work the process. Not everybody is ready to repent of their sins and be redeemed. Not everybody is ready for an extreme makeover of their hearts or their heads. Remember the verse stated, *"...be transformed by the renewing of your mind."* Bottom-line – **The Refinement Process** works as you allow the process to work in you. This success is available to whosoever will cooperate with the grace of the Refiner and Redeemer.

For the grace of God that bringeth salvation hath appeared to all men, Teaching us that, denying ungodliness and worldly lusts, we should live soberly, righteously, and godly, in this present world; Looking for that blessed hope, and the glorious appearing of the great God and our Savior Jesus Christ; Who gave himself for us, **that he might redeem us from all iniquity, and purify unto himself** *a peculiar people, zealous of good works.* Titus 2:11-14

Release and Relief

Here, at the Redemption Station, you find both release and relief. Addictions come with chains of slavery. They wrap themselves all around you. From your head to your feet, the chains of addiction bind your thinking; they bind your emotions and your motivations. Addictions even restricted your mobility, both physically and mentally. They especially bind your upward mobility. Where could you go in the advancement of your education and career if you were without the chains of addiction?

Through redemption, the Refiner has released you from every limitation, hindrance, barrier, pitfall and trap. Released from every addiction!

In addition to release, He gives you relief. There is always much pain and sorrow attached to addictions. Broken relationships, broken homes, broken careers, broken health, broken finances; these are painful and sorrowful reminders of your broken-down life with drugs.

Relief is here! Even the smallest sliver or thorn embedded in your finger causes pain in your whole body. Once the thorn of addiction is removed, there is relief in your whole body, mind and spirit.

Let's look at the life of a woman who found release and relief.
NOTE: Due to the sensitive nature of this story the names of family members have been changed to protect their privacy.

The Regina Goethe Story

"I'm not dead" I cried, "I'm alive!" A cry first made in anguish at twelve years old, now made in joy!

I was abandoned at the hospital two days after my birth. Because my father was absent and my mother snuck off, I could not be adopted and became a ward of the state, destined to a long string of foster care homes where I would be abused and raped. Many times I ran away, but I was always found and returned.

At the age of twelve, the courts ordered that I be moved to another city to an emergency foster care home to protect me from the continual rapes. I was placed in the home of a devout Christian woman who made sure I was in church several times a week. I rebelled because I was not used to church, but there, in church, I had a profound religious experience the memory of which would serve as my rescue in years to come.

During a revival church service, the pastor began to speak to the congregation about a girl whom the Lord loved. A special girl who had suffered much abuse, had never known love, felt abandoned and uncared for so much so that she desired suicide, but God had not allow her to do it.

How dare he tell all of my personal business in front of the church? I don't know him and he certainly don't know me! I thought, sure he was telling my story.

I began cursing out the pastor, my foster mother, and everybody else in the church. I felt fully exposed in front of strangers. I had learned to bury and cover up all of my pain and shame; nobody was supposed to know about my deep dark past. In tears, I ran out of the church. I was flush with anger and shame, but I was brought back into the building where the pastor tried to encourage me.

"Sweetheart, the Lord loves you and he wants you to know it. And to prove He loves you, the Lord told me to tell you to ask Him for anything your heart desires and He will give it to you."

More than anything, my secret desire was to know my biological family. I wanted to know who I really was. I wanted somebody to love me, really love me, and I dreamed they would. But, I angrily retorted, "I don't believe in God! What kind of god would allow all of those evil things to happen to me?"

My response brought a swift, equally angry response from my foster mother. That night I got the whipping of my life. But I didn't care; I was used to whippings. Later that same night, after my foster mother went to sleep, I got out the Stanford (my hometown) telephone book and started looking up people with my same last name. I found five names. I dialed the first number and began playing cruel pranks on the person. Before I ended the call I cursed her out. I went on to the next number and repeated the process. Down the list of numbers I proceeded until my foster mother awoke and picked up the phone receiver. She heard me pranking on the phone. She apologized to the woman on the phone and tried to explain to her the reason for my bad behavior. In her explanation, she mentioned my name Regina Goethe.

The woman on the call became hysterical and accused my foster mother of playing a sick, cruel trick.

"Who did you talk to Terry, Christina or someone in my family? Who told you about Regina? Everybody knows that my granddaughter

Regina Goethe died at birth! Why are you doing this to me?" she screamed.

"I'm not dead! I'm alive!" I screamed in to the phone.

At three in the morning, in my foster mother's living room, I met members of my biological family; a family I had not known existed. My grandmother, my aunts and my sister all had rushed to see this child whom they thought was dead. Only my mother was missing.

Several days later I met Aunt Quiana. I was amazed by her beauty. She was the prettiest lady I had ever seen, finely dressed, with long hair. Weeks later, my sister secretly confided to me, "Regina, Aunt Quiana is really your mother."

I began to cry. So many thoughts flooded my mind. What was the matter with me? Why didn't anyone want me? Why was the whole family together except me? All of them have such nice lives. But look at me, my life is a mess. I am a mess.

I found no answers and I remained in foster care for another full year before my mother took custody of me and moved me into her home. Little did I know that I was falling out of the frying pan and into the fire. My new stepfather hated me, angrily telling me that to my face. Over the months he physically abused me, beating me unmercifully, until my badly bruised body was noticed at school and the guidance counselor called the police and social services. But when the counselor left the room, I fled the school, knowing that I would be returned to foster care.

Oddly, I finally found acceptance with the other teenage street people; the drug people with whom I chose to live. They became my new family. We ate, slept, boozed and got high together, smoking weed and snorting cocaine. Over time, an older man took an interest in caring for me, taking me under his wing and showing me kindness and affection. He taught me how to dress and how to respect myself. I eventually got a job and we found an apartment.

With good food, booze and plenty of cocaine, our place became the hangout for all our druggie friends. We both held jobs, working hard and *playing* hard. Two daughters were born of our relationship. Even when our relationship ended, I continued to work and support my girls.

Over the years I became a functioning cocaine addict. I was a *closet* addict. Many of my acquaintances never suspected that I was a drug addict. Then came crack, the new pure and powerful solid form of cocaine. For me, that was the beginning of the end. My addictions could no longer be hidden; I became a crackhead.

The bills were paid late, if at all. The phone was cut off, the rent was overdue, and I became lax in caring for my children. I lost my apartment and started shifting my family from shelter to shelter. My life was out of control. My children suffered as their mother was no longer their strong protector and provider. If I got $20, two dollars went for Ramen Noodles and the rest went for crack. One night, as I looked over my shambled life, I had an epiphany.

"Lord," I said, "I remember You. I knew You as a little kid. I remember that You told me to ask whatever my heart's desire and you would give it to me. And You didn't wait for the next day, that same night you gave me my family. I know that You are real! So we have to have a serious talk. I hate everything about my life. I wish I was dead, but You won't even let me kill myself. There were times when I put so much crack on my pipe that it should have busted my heart. I should be dead. I wake up every day not knowing why I'm still alive. So here's the deal, I need for You to help me. I need for You to show me how to get past all of this pain."

Indeed, God sent me help. An apostle came to my door urging me to go to church, but the devil wasn't done with me yet. I ignored the invitation to go to church and instead gathered my friends for a night of beer and drugs. I recall drinking and smoking crack. As I was raising the pipe to my lips for another hit I heard an audible voice.

"If you take that hit you shall surely die!"

It scared me so badly; I thought I had gone crazy. The pipe flew out of my hand one way and the crack flew the other way. Still stunned, I again heard the voice say,

"I am providing a way for you. Now, you get up, you and your kids, and get to that church right now!"

I gathered my girls, got a neighbor to drive me to a church, and took a seat at the very back of the room. Thinking they were expecting me, after all God had sent me, I was surprised and shamed as I overheard some of the ladies talking.

"Look at that! How dare she come in the house of God like that? Look at how high she is. Some people have no respect. That's a shame!"

But, that did not deter me. They didn't know that God had interrupted my party and had sent me there. All I wanted was to be rescued and to be safe. In that church, for the first time in my life, I accepted Jesus. More than ever, I became hungry to know God.

My deliverance from drugs did not happen overnight. It was a gradual process which had a humbling effect on me. I was being refined and prepared for the purpose the Lord had intended from the start. I was determined to attend church, even though I was still getting high. Each high carried a conviction that I needed more of the supernatural power of God to deliver me.

"Lord, will I ever be through with this addiction?" I asked. "I just want to be pure."

Before my deliverance from drugs, I would go into the crack houses with my Bible and a crack pipe. I would pick up the crack pipe saying, "I may not be able to let this go, but I refuse to let this go!" and clutch my Bible. Ironically, after everybody got high, they would ask me questions about Jesus. It was like everybody wanted to know about the Lord.

Regina came through the Refinery and now she is a changed woman. No longer bound by drug addictions; at last Regina was freed. Today she has compassion for people who are addicted to drugs. She told her story in hopes of encouraging someone to get the help that they need.

Regina's advice: Don't give up. Don't give in. Don't let go of God. No matter how long it takes, always believe and trust Him. No matter how desperate you are. Yes, there will be some desperate times, and yes, you will find yourself at your most lowly state, but God will meet you there. He has a time and He has a way. I thank God for all of my experiences because they taught me and they humbled me. The things that hurt me the most have given me compassion and patience for other people. They remind me that God is phenomenal and such an awesome God. No matter what your personal story is, He has an awesome ending for you; and at the ending of it, He will be glorified!

The Boy Who Lost His Boat

Tom carried his new toy boat to the edge of the river. He carefully placed it in the water and slowly let out the string. How smoothly the boat sailed! Tom sat in the warm sunshine, admiring the little boat that he had built. Suddenly a strong current caught the boat. Tom tried to pull it back to shore, but the string broke. The little boat raced downstream.

Tom ran along the sandy shore as fast as he could. But his little boat soon slipped out of sight. All afternoon he searched for the boat. Finally, when it was too dark to look any longer, Tom sadly went home.

A few days later, on the way home from school, Tom spotted a boat just like his in a store window. When he got closer, he could see -

- sure enough -- it was his! Tom hurried to the store manager. "Sir, that's my boat in your window! I made it!"

"Sorry, son, but someone else brought it in this morning. If you want it, you'll have to buy it for ten dollars."

Tom ran home and counted all his money. Exactly ten dollars! When he reached the store, he rushed to the counter. "Here's the money for my boat." As he left the store, Tom hugged his boat and said, "Now you're twice mine. First, I made you and now I bought you." [17]

In creation, Jesus made you. In redemption, He bought you back!

Action Step 2

Based on the Refiner's perspective of you that you discovered in Action Step 1, let's summarize:

You are fearfully and wonderfully created to look like Him (His image) and to act like Him (His likeness).

You are created for His pleasure.

You are created to be productive and powerful, to be fruitful, multiply, replenish, subdue, and have dominion over His creation.

You are to avoid the dead-end roads which falsely appear to be the right way.

You are created to reign with Him throughout eternity.

Now, put this together to create a power Vision Statement for your everyday life and your future.

I (your name) am fearfully and wonderfully created by God to look like Him and to act like Him. He created me for His pleasure. I (your name) am created to be productive and powerful.

I (your name) do that by being fruitful, multiplying the resources of my fruitfulness, then using those multiplied resources for the replenishing of people.

My Refiner is always with me and He always points me to the right path. Through Him, I (your name) make use of the supernatural power available to me.

Write this Vision Statement on a card and carry it with you in your wallet or purse or tape it on your bathroom mirror. Print it on a poster board and hang it up in your room. Read it and speak it often. This statement, my friend, is the essence of who you are and why you are on this planet! You exist to bring glory to God. This is the reason why the Refiner wants to refine you. And this will last forever-if you are redeemed by the Refiner's blood.

Redemption Review Platform

Redemption is deliverance by the payment of a price; it is rescue from the grip of addictions, and much, much more.

The Refiner, Lord Jesus, (who never sinned) was crucified in order to pay the price for your sins.

Your Heart is your Believer, Your Head is your Thinker.
Trust in the Lord with all your **heart**.
Be transformed by the renewing of your **mind.**

Through redemption the Refiner:
Released you from every limitation, hindrance, barrier, pitfall, and trap.
Released you from every addiction!

In creation, Jesus made you.
In redemption, He bought you back!

Staging Area Four

Wow! **The Refinement Process** has been a truly amazing journey. But we are not through yet. There are still two critical stations through which you must pass. I am sure you are starting to see and feel the results of the Refiner's hands upon you. You are made FREE!

In preparation for the Recommitment Station, it is time to take a quick inventory. Please take a few moments to answer the following questions:

1. When was the last time you broke a promise? Explain.
2. When was the last time you kept a promise? Explain.
3. Is it easier for you to tell the truth or to lie?
4. What must you do to remain committed to the Refiner?

During the Reflection Station and Repentance Station you were in charge. First, you saw a reflection of the real you. Second, you went on to confess your iniquities (impurities) and asked for forgiveness and deliverance from your addictions.

In the Redemption Station, the Refiner took charge. He turned up The Refinery fire to cleanse you from all unrighteousness and release you from the chains of your addictions. He sacrificed His own life so you could have a more abundant and eternal life.

Now, in the Recommitment Station, the charge returns to you. The completeness of your deliverance will be your responsibility and it will require your firm commitments. You must fill your new life with the things which please God. Reexamine your Vision Statement from Action Step 2 in the Redemption Station. You must make it the blueprint for constructing your successful, meaningful, purposeful life. It will be challenging, but with your powerful Refiner always present, you have all you need to succeed. The Refiner's purpose combined with your plan, that's a winning combo.

There is a warning sign at the entrance to the Recommitment Station. It states:

> **Guard Your Heart For Out Of It Flows the Streams Of Your Life**

The Recommitment Station

Recommitment: to commit again.

Into your hands I commit my spirit; deliver me, LORD, my faithful God. Psalms 31:5 (NIV)

My Story

Over the months prior to my relocation, Marva and I had maintained a long-distant friendship. We talked frequently on the telephone and we exchanged letters every few days. Her encouraging letters brought me through some dark days. I loved to receive her letters, lavender envelopes containing matching lavender stationary with her perfect lettering, accented with just a touch of her most exquisite perfume. I always knew when her letters were in my mailbox; oh, what a wonderful scent. Through the phone calls and letters we grew closer even though we lived far from each other.

On that fateful July 5th afternoon, with just a duffle-bag and my guitar, I boarded the Trailways bus headed to Rochester. I left my stuff in Boston. Not only had I left my physical possessions there, but I also left all my *stuff*, you know, the excess baggage we all carry. For me, it was critical to make a clean break with my past, the people, the places and the possessions.

When I arrived in Rochester I didn't have a pot to pee in. I moved into my parents' house on Brooks Avenue and settled into the spare bedroom in the attic. Fortunately for me, I was on good terms with my folks. There were other bridges that I had foolishly burned in the past, but not so with my folks. In fact, it was a great, positive, and supportive environment. It was a place where I could be reconnected with my life prior to the interruption of drugs. I relished the love and acceptance of Dad and Mom.

With the reconnection also came the need to recommit my life to relatives and, especially, to the Refiner. His work was still under way as I moved through His Refinery. He was creating for me an environment where drugs did not fit. My primary focus became trusting in Him. My sole purpose became submitting myself to Him. I know that that sounds corny, definitely not cool. But at that point in my life being cool didn't seem too cool.

For many years I had lived the way I thought was cool. Where did it get me? I was on the bottom looking up. Now, I had the opportunity to see my upside down life turned right-side up. For me, being cool had caused me to be a fool. No thanks, I was done with cool; I was ready to commit. Now the question for you is - Are you ready to commit?

Stay on Course – Stay Committed

It is extremely important that you stay committed to the Refiner. **The Refinement Process** is here to help you do that. Without commitment, your power to stay the course will be diminished. It was He who rescued you; it will be He who keeps you safe during impending pains and persecutions. He has promised He will never leave you nor forget about you.

The Refiner is that constant help you will need in order to succeed in your new addiction free life. Think back on the mess you created for yourself in the past. Now that you are being delivered from your past failures, it is crucial for you to maintain your victorious life without drugs. The Recommitment Station will help you in this maintenance.

You will be facing many trials, testings and temptations. Your natural body will have a longing to go back to the old ways. You are in the process of cleansing and purification, and, yet, your mind and body will sometimes long for past drug highs. You must remember how low those drug highs brought you.

As a dog returns to its vomit, so fools repeat their folly. Proverbs 26:11 NIV

It's time for you to recommit to yourself and to your loved ones. In this process of recommitment, you will need to *de-commit* to your old negative people, places, and so-called pleasures. There are two types of commitments, or, it might be better said, two directions of commitments, horizontal and vertical. Let's look at how these commitments affect your new life.

Horizontal and Vertical Commitments

The word horizontal is defined as: relating to, directed toward, or consisting of individuals or entities of similar status or on the same level. The word vertical is defined as: situated at the highest point. But, what does that have to do with commitments? Let's examine this concept.

Horizontal Commitments are your commitments to people on your same level. These are the commitments that you make to your friends and family, your co-workers or your fellow students. These are what could be called peer to peer commitments.

Horizontal Commitments also refer to the type of commitment between married couples and soul-mates. Sororities and fraternities, civic groups (Rotary or Lions), fraternal orders (Elks, Shriners or Masons) all require high standards of commitment. Horizontal Commitments are reciprocal. You commit to others and you expect the same degree of commitment from them in return.

On the other side, Vertical Commitments are your commitments to those people of higher authority. These are the commitments you make to your parents, your workplace supervisor, your teachers or professors, and your pastor or spiritual leaders.

Vertical Commitments are the basis of what is known as the chain of command. You see it in all branches of the military and in business enterprises both small and large. All people have to answer to those of higher ranking or in higher authority. And again, just like with Horizontal Commitments, Vertical Commitments are reciprocal. There is an expectation of commitment from those of lower ranking as well as from those of higher ranking.

The highest Vertical Commitments of all are those we make to Jesus the Refiner. We commit ourselves to love, honor, and obey Him. We commit ourselves to let His will have priority over our will. Jesus said it best when He prioritized the will of His heavenly Father over His own will. In Luke 22:42 Jesus said, *Father, if thou be willing, remove this cup from me* (referring to Christ's mission to redeem us by His death on a cross). He went on to say, *nevertheless not my will but thine be done*. It was the ultimate Vertical Commitment, and it should be our pledge to God, our heavenly Father; **not my will, but Your will be done**. That becomes proof of your devotion to Him.

> **Higher levels of commitment require**
> **Deeper levels of devotion to God**

Your commitment to the Refiner is your most important commitment of all. The Refiner gave you His promises. Keep your word to Him by remembering His words to you.

Vowing a Vow

Your commitment is your promise, your pledge, your oath, your word, your vow. The words pledge, oath, and vow are synonymous. They represent an oral contract of performance. A vow is a spoken agreement between two or more people. Vowing a vow is the act of pledging or promising that you will do something for the person.

There are many examples of vowing a vow. You see it when a politician takes the Oath of Office, vowing to be a leader for his constituents. When you Pledge Allegiance to the flag, you vow to be loyal to the United States of America. When couples exchange wedding vows, they promise to be faithful and care for each other. Priests might take a vow of celibacy, or a vow of poverty, or a vow of silence, all to bring them closer to God. Vows are the basis of a commitment that binds together relationships.

A vow is constructed of four basic building blocks – the People, the Pledge, the Prize and the Payment. You can see that it is similar to any business or personal transaction. Whether it's a sales contract or its loaning money to a friend, a vow incorporates the 4 Ps: the People, the Pledge, the Prize and the Payment. Let's examine this further.

The People are the two or more persons coming into an agreement through the vow. On one side is the person(s) who vows the vow (makes the pledge) and on the other side is the person(s) who provides the prize (the desired results or desired object.)

The Pledge is simply your word. When vowing a vow, your pledge is your verbal promise to accomplish something in exchange for a desired result or a desired object. In most cases, the vow is verbal, spoken in the presence of the other person with whom you are in agreement.

The Prize is the object of your desire or the results that you desire in exchange for the payment of your vows.

The Payment is the actual performance of the pledge. The person making the vow has to do the thing which he or she pledged to do.

This whole process can be understood in the following example. **I pledge allegiance to the flag of the United States of America, and to the republic for which it stands, one nation under God, indivisible, with liberty and justice for all.** From classrooms and school auditoriums to political rallies and major sports events, many people address the Stars and Stripes and repeat this vow. Look at the 4 Ps in this example.

- The People – citizens of the United States of America
- The Pledge – allegiance to the flag and the republic
- The Prize – one indivisible nation with liberty and justice for all
- The Payment – devotion to this nation and an obligation to be loyal to it

Generally, the prize is given before the payment is made. When the prize is provided, there is an expectation of the payment. If the prize is received and the payment is not performed, there is injustice and imbalance. A person enjoys gain while the other person suffers loss. The Lord, our Refiner requires justice and balance in your relationships. He takes vows very seriously. He expects fulfillment of the pledge and payment for the prize.

That which has gone from your lips you shall keep and perform, for you voluntarily vowed to the LORD your God what you have promised with your mouth. Deuteronomy 23:23 (NKJV)

When you make a vow to God, do not delay to pay it; For He has no pleasure in fools. Pay what you have vowed - Better not to vow than to vow and not pay. Do not let your mouth cause your flesh to sin… Ecclesiastes 5:4-6a (NKJV)

A word to the wise concerning vows; if you can't pay it, then don't say it. Always pay your vows.

Action Step 1

Drug addicts lack integrity. But in the freedom you have from the Refiner, you can now have integrity in your character. Start small, but build your integrity through making and fulfilling vows. Now let's practice vowing a vow. Make it simple and doable; don't promise something that is not within your ability to perform.

1. Prepare a vow to the Refiner. Think of one significant vow to the Lord.
2. Print the vow. Print or write out your vow.
3. Proclaim the vow. Verbally state the pledge to the Lord to whom you make the vow.
4. Post the vow. Find a prominent place in your home to post your vow.

Remember, always pay your vows, especially to the Lord. If you can't pay it, then don't say it.

> **Your vows should be Prepared, Printed, Proclaimed and Posted.**

Your vows (promises) are important. Record and review them until they become ingrained in your spirit. Remember, your word gains value when you keep it!

> **Your word Appreciates (gains value) when you keep it.**
> **Your word Depreciates (loses value) when you break it.**

Refinement Hero

Ruth was a young woman from the land of Moab. She met and married Chilion, the son of Naomi and Elimelech, who were emigrants from Judea. Over the course of time Elimelech and his son Chilion died, leaving Naomi and Ruth as grieving widows.

Naomi decided to leave Moab and return to her relatives in land of Judea, because she had no means of supporting herself. Having decided to go it alone, she bid farewell to her daughter-in-law, Ruth. But Ruth refused to depart. She had other plans. Ruth decided to remain with her mother-in-law, Naomi, and accompany her back to Judea, a land Ruth had never seen.

The move would make Ruth a foreigner in Judea. Knowing that she faced an uncertain future, Ruth vowed a vow to Naomi. Ruth's vow epitomizes the concept of commitment. These are the words of her vow to Naomi:

Don't urge me to leave you or to turn back from you. Where you go I will go, and where you stay I will stay. Your people will be my people and your God my God. Where you die I will die, and there I will be buried. May the LORD deal with me, be it ever so severely, if even death separates you and me. Ruth 1:16-17 (NIV)

WOW! That almost sounds like wedding vows. Ruth's love and dedication caused her to reach down to the depths of her soul and swear the oath to Naomi. Your own commitments, both horizontal and vertical, should have the same strength and depth. In the past, your commitments may have been weak and shallow, but now is the time for you to strongly and deeply pledge your commitments to your family, to yourself, and to your Refiner.

Could you vow a vow like that to your supporters? Could you make that level of commitment to yourself to live each day to the fullest and to be the best you can be? Could you make a strong vow like that to the Refiner?

As they returned to the Judean countryside, Ruth made good on her vows to Naomi. Ruth found work as a field laborer and supported herself and Naomi with her proceeds. Ruth stuck by Naomi and never wavered from her pledge. People took notice of her and she gained the respect of the whole community of Bethlehem.

The Lord honored Ruth's vow to Naomi and caused them both to prosper. Ruth remained committed and because of her commitment, the Lord prepared and positioned Ruth to become the wife of Boaz, a very prosperous landowner. It all began with a deep commitment between two women.

> **The depth of your commitment will determine the height of your success.**

My Story

With great excitement I anticipated seeing Marva again. But, there remained some unfinished business between us concerning my pledge to her and my commitment to keep that pledge. Remember Marva's challenge to me: *You can be with me or you can be with your drugs but you can't have us both, you decide.* The fact that I chose to be with Marva was the motivation that propelled me into The Refinery. The key, at that point, was recommitment.

"Hey, Marva. I'm back home in Rochester."

"Oh, hi Ron, it's good to hear from you."

"I made my decision. I want to be with you. I left the drugs in Boston. I'm drug-free." I said with very little confidence.

"That's nice," she said, also lacking confidence, but willing to watch and see.

"You'll see," I said with a little more boldness. "I'm living here with my parents. I think this will be good for me, initially. At least until I can get a job. I would like to see you."

"Ron, remember you promised absolutely no drugs, right?"

"That's right Marva. No more drugs."

"If you're not busy you can come over tonight."

"I'll see you tonight."

My recommitment to Marva required more than just showing up on her doorstep. I needed to pledge my total commitment to keep drugs out of our relationship. That night, I gladly made my pledge to her that I would remain drug-free. With watchful eyes she accepted my pledge. She believed me, but over the following months she also paid close attention to my progress.

The time had come for me to put action to my words. The Refiner made good on His commitment to me. He totally delivered me from drug addiction. My part of the agreement was to commit to live a drug-free life. I renewed my pledge to Him which I first stated back in the Repentance Station; *I surrender to You, please take these drugs out of my life.* With the same intensity I used to have to get high, I directed myself toward my purification as a result of **The Refinement Process**.

My Horizontal Commitment to Marva would not have been possible if I had not already made my Vertical Commitment to the Refiner. Together, the vertical and horizontal commitments are like the vertical and horizontal wooden beams which made up the crucifixion cross of Christ, our Refiner.

Over the months, we fell in love and I asked her to be my wife and accept my marriage vows. We made plans to be married the following June. But, even the best of intentions can sometimes get detoured. Regrettably, I had two brief relapses before I finally and totally realized my freedom. I will explain later about my detour on the Relapse Road.

Stay Perfected – Stay Pure

The Bible, in the book of 1 Corinthians 6:19 (NLT), teaches that *your body is the temple of the Holy Spirit, who lives in you*. It goes on in the next verse to state *...you must honor God with your body*. This tells us we have a responsibility to stay loyal and to stay pure. How do you honor God with your body? You honor Him when you take good care of your body, which is His property.

Have you ever had somebody visit you at your home and leave it a mess? Have you ever loaned something valuable to a friend and have it returned dirty or broken? Of course. We all from time to time experience somebody who has absolutely no respect for our possessions. When they disrespect your possessions, they, in effect, disrespect you. How does that make you feel?

Now, think about the Refiner's claim that your body is His temple. He instructed you to honor it. Are you a person who leaves it a mess? Are you a person who returns it dirty or damaged? If that's you, fix it! Do not leave God's property in worse condition than the way you received it. You received it, at birth, perfected and pure. You damaged it through drug abuse and addictions. But, through The Refinery and **The Refinement Process**, your heart can be restored to perfection and purity.

In 1982, First Lady Nancy Reagan was asked by an Oakland California schoolgirl what she would do if somebody offered her drugs. Mrs. Reagan responded, "Just say no!" That became the catchphrase for President Reagan's War on Drugs. Well, the war was lost; drugs won. That campaign showed us that to *Just Say No* was not enough to defeat drugs. It takes commitment.

To say, *Stay Perfect and Stay Pure,* will not win the battle. Catchphrases are not enough. To win this campaign requires your unwavering commitment. Remember the price the Refiner paid for your ransom. He suffered extreme persecution, pain, and a torturous execution to pay for your rescue and redemption. He paid a debt He did not owe so that you could receive salvation you did not deserve. Recognize that now you are His. Use your life to honor Him.

Never forget, you don't have to do it alone. You have with you at all times a supernatural power available to you. The Refiner is always there to help you maintain. Make a commitment to God to strive to stay perfect and pure. He is committed to you; after all, He also wants His temple clean! If this all seems impossible, you are right. For mankind it is impossible, but with God all things are possible. Impossibilities are no match for the Refiner's supernatural power which He makes available to you.

Action Step 2

Earlier in this Recommitment Station I told you how and why I left my stuff behind when I relocated to Rochester. It was important for me to make a break with my addicted life. For me it represented a new, fresh start. That was my stuff - MY stuff.

There is a problem when your stuff isn't really YOUR stuff. It might be misappropriated stuff (stolen) or it might be stuff borrowed and never returned. Either way, it is stuff that is not rightfully yours. It is difficult starting your new life with stuff that belongs to someone else.

So, for this Action Step you will jettison (get rid of cargo) other people's stuff. Start by taking inventory of all of your stuff. Make notes or tag stuff that you recognize is not yours: public library books from 1995, Nikes that still have the price tag on them, power tools with your neighbor's initials engraved in the side; you know the stuff. Separate other people's stuff from your stuff.

Now take one (or all) of the following actions:
- Return borrowed stuff
- Restore stolen stuff
- Repay your debts
- Make good on past promises

Do these things and you will feel so much better about your own stuff and about yourself. Other people will feel better about you too! It is a win-win situation. There may be stuff that you cannot return, restore, or repay. In those cases, maybe you can compensate in other ways using your time or talent in service to them. Do your best to return, restore, repay, and make good on past promises. Obviously, these actions will take some time to complete, so get started and get it done.

Recommitment Review Platform

Horizontal is defined as: relating to, directed toward, or consisting of individuals or entities of similar status or on the same level.
Vertical is defined as: situated at the highest point.

Horizontal Commitments are made to other people.
Vertical Commitments are made to the Refiner, Lord Jesus.

A Vow requires the 4 Ps:
- The People
- The Pledge
- The Prize and
- The Payment

Your vows need to be:
- Prepared
- Printed
- Proclaimed and
- Posted

Higher Levels of Commitment Require Deeper Levels of Devotion.

The Height of Your Success will be Determined by The Depth of Your Commitment.

Your word Appreciates (gains value) when you keep it.
Your word Depreciates (loses value) when you break it.

Staging Area Five

Here you are! You have reached the last station in The Refinery.

The time has come for you to get up and get started in your new life. But be cautious; do not start something new the same old way! Start your new life with a new and improved perspective, a new mindset where drugs do not fit.

Jesus, the Refiner died and was buried as sin. He arose, the victorious Son of God. His reemergence occurred when He rose from the dead. That is your model (pattern) for reemergence: death, burial, and resurrection. In The Refinery, you were buried as a planted seed. Once the seed falls into fertile ground, the outer shell begins to open as it dies, and inside the dead shell, new life emerges. The seed had to die in the ground to produce a plant. Your old life died and now you will emerge as a productive person. From this Reemergence Station you will be seen as a new creation, born anew.

Talk with the Refiner every day. Daily tell Him,

"O Lord, my Refiner, transform my tastes. Adjust my appetite for things that are wholesome. Reform my soul. Purge me of the unrighteous pleasure of sin. Let me not be entertained or amused by sinful acts. I renounce spiritual wickedness that has influenced my tastes. Your perfect strength applies to my every weakness."

Always remember, you did not rescue yourself, the Refiner rescued you. Be grateful to Him for saving you. Be thankful to Him for your new purified life. Now that you have been delivered from drug dependency, remember to glorify God.

One of them, when he saw he was healed, came back, praising God in a loud voice. He threw himself at Jesus' feet and thanked him—and he was a Samaritan. Jesus asked, "Were not all ten cleansed? Where are the other nine? Has no one returned to give praise to God except this foreigner?" Then he said to him, "Rise and go; your faith has made you well." Luke 17:15-19 (NIV)

The Bible said that when Jesus cleansed the ten lepers, only one man came back, fell down at His feet and thanked Him. Just like the one leprous man who was cleansed, it is important for you to go to the Refiner and give Him thanks. He appreciates being appreciated!

In the Reemergence Station, you will learn how to maintain your sobriety. You do so by staging your new life, removing the old patterns of behavior and replacing them with new, positive behaviors

My friend, let's walk into your new life. Enter the Reemergence Station.

The Reemergence Station

Reemergence: the act or process of emerging again; Evolution - the appearance of new properties or species in the course of development.

I am forgotten as a dead man out of mind: I am like a broken vessel.
Psalms 31:12

Refinement Hero

God called the Prophet Jonah to go into Nineveh, a foreign country, and to tell them about their impending destruction if they failed to repent. Jonah disobeyed and set out to go in the opposite direction. He hated the people of Nineveh and he did not want them to be saved. Therefore, he fled from the presence of the Lord.

Jonah paid the fare and departed on a ship sailing to Tarshish. God told him to go to Nineveh, but Jonah decided instead to go to Tarshish. Have you ever done that? Have you ever gone in the opposite direction from the place where God told you to go? I have!

It wasn't long before the ship was engulfed in a fierce storm. The strong winds and the high waves threatened the ship as they beat against it. The crew began throwing the cargo overboard attempting to lighten the load. But the storm continued to rage. In desperation, the sailors began praying to their foreign gods. Their situation was hopeless and their gods were useless. They finally confronted Jonah who confessed to them that he was to be blamed for the storm. He told them he was running away from the Lord of heaven and earth.

The sailors then began to pray to the Lord and to plead for their lives. Imagine that; at first they prayed to their pagan gods, but they finally prayed to the Lord God. Their prayers were answered as they obeyed instructions to throw Jonah overboard. As soon as they jettisoned Jonah, the storm ceased and they were saved.

On the other hand, Jonah was sinking to the bottom of the sea! But God had other plans. In fact, God was sticking to His original plan for Jonah to go to Nineveh. God prepared a great fish to swallow up Jonah and to carry him to his destination. The once prideful Jonah was in the belly of the fish for three days and three nights. Look at Jonah's humble words as he soaked in the stinking gut of a fish in total darkness:

> *"In trouble, deep trouble, I prayed to God. He answered me.*
> *From the belly of the grave I cried, 'Help!' You heard my cry.*
> *You threw me into ocean's depths, into a watery grave,*
> *With ocean waves, ocean breakers crashing over me.*
> *I said, 'I've been thrown away, thrown out, out of your sight.*
> *I'll never again lay eyes on your Holy Temple.'*
> *Ocean gripped me by the throat.*
> *The ancient Abyss grabbed me and held tight.*
> *My head was all tangled in seaweed*
> *at the bottom of the sea where the mountains take root.*
> *I was as far down as a body can go,*
> *and the gates were slamming shut behind me forever -*
> *Yet you pulled me up from that grave alive, O GOD, my God!*
> *When my life was slipping away, I remembered GOD,*
> *And my prayer got through to you, made it all the way to your Holy Temple.*
> *Those who worship hollow gods, god-frauds, walk away from their only true love.*
> *But I'm worshiping you, God, calling out in thanksgiving!*
> *And I'll do what I promised I'd do! Salvation belongs to God!"*
> *Then GOD spoke to the fish, and it vomited up Jonah on the seashore.*

Jonah 2:1-10 (MSG)

Now, that's what I call reemergence! When Jonah had a change of heart, the Refiner gave him a change in direction. At the point of certain death, the Refiner brought Jonah out in to a new life.

Out of the Cocoon

The Refinery is like the belly of Jonah's great fish. It will help you to refocus your life on God. Like a gold refinery, it will melt you down and cause the impurities to rise to the surface for removal. This Refinery is also like a cocoon. You enter as a creeping, crawling caterpillar, symbolic of your old, low and slow way of living. You proceed through **The Refinement Process** and you are totally transformed from the inside out. You are emerging, out of the cocoon, as a fully developed, beautiful butterfly, a colorful Monarch. Now that you have come out, there is no longer a need to crawl; it is time to fly. Stretch out your wings; you are going up. Reemerge better than ever.

Do not return to the old mess which was your old life. Do not go back to that old environment. Jonah never returned to the belly of the fish. When Jesus arose from the dead, He never returned to the empty tomb. The butterfly doesn't go back to the cocoon out of which it came. Neither does the butterfly associate with caterpillars. Get out and fly with other butterflies!

You have set yourselves a difficult task, but you will succeed if you persevere; and you will find a joy in overcoming obstacles. Helen Keller

Visibility Restored

As an addict, you were out of sight. You were hidden; you were invisible. Why? Because nobody really wanted to see you. You were too big a mess. You messed over people. Family, neighbors, friends, co-workers, they were all stained by your addictions. Consequently, many of them erased you from their sight.

Now that you are purified, you will shine so brightly, people will have to notice you. The new you!

> **It is wiser to change surroundings than to let surroundings change you.**

People will recognize a change in you. Some people will like the change, some people will hate it. Those who like your positive change will be those who will be an encouragement to you. They will be supportive of your growth and development. Try to surround yourself with those people. This will probably require you to enclose around yourself a new circle of friends, letting go of old counter-productive relationships.

People who hate the positive changes in you will want you to go back to your old ways. They will miss having you there with them. Remember the old saying: misery loves company. Just make sure that you do not become the person that misery loves. By any means necessary, avoid former acquaintances who are still addicted. No matter how much you love them, or enjoy being around them, druggies will not fit into your new life, so don't even try to make room for them.

At this stage of your development, you are not ready to debate or defend your new life free from addictive drugs. Some of your old friends and associates will not understand it and many of them will not like the fact that you have escaped from their disastrous fate. Give yourself plenty of time to grow and develop in your new life. The Refiner has given you a better way to live. Enjoy it and make the most of it.

Control Your Environment

The federal government has a department whose sole mission is to protect the environment. The Environmental Protection Agency

(EPA) monitors, regulates and enforces laws concerning Land, Air, and Water Pollution.

If the federal government considers it important to protect the environment, why is it that people do not think it important enough to protect their own personal environment? I do not mean your land, air or water; I refer to the protection of your mind, heart and soul. You should establish your own Personal Environmental Protection policies (PEPs). You must diligently protect your own personal environment. You must monitor, regulate, and enforce the laws concerning your life space, your personal environment.

Just to be clear, I am not referring to air or water pollution. By Personal Environmental Protection, I am referring to your living and working space. You may ask, "How do I protect my own environment?" You protect your Personal Environment by first identifying the pollutants in your space. Pollutants come in the form of polluted pressures, polluted people or polluted paraphernalia.

Polluted Pressures – Defile your Character
Polluted People – Corrupt your Thinking
Polluted Paraphernalia – Disable your Actions

Polluted Pressures

Daily, you face external forces that put downward pressure on you. I call them Polluted Pressures. These hindering forces are all around you, and, if you are not cautious, they can negatively impact your new refined life. There is a proverb which states,

Above all else, guard your heart, for everything you do flows from it. Proverbs 4:23 (NIV)

Polluted Pressures are exhibited in the music, movies, television, and negative talk that surrounds you each day. These are vehicles which regularly deliver filth to your heart.

Lyrics, which stir up your lusts; movies, which glorify alcohol and drug abuse; discussions, which ridicule and revile God; the Polluted Pressures are all around you.

God instructs you to be aware of what you permit into your heart. You need to place a guard at your Eye-Gate and your Ear-Gate. Think about it: Much of what you see and hear is polluted. Those things will defile your character. The Refiner purified your heart and He is in the process of perfecting you. He expects you to keep it clean. Therefore, it is crucial that your Personal Environmental Protection policies include your policy to identify and avoid Polluted Pressures.

One of the habits I practice which helps me to protect my environment is attending church. Through regular church attendance you can be strengthened in your relationship with the Refiner. Ask the Refiner for help in this area. He will lead and guide you in all truth. If regularly attending church is your course of action, make sure you go to a Bible believing, Bible teaching church. Look at their Mission Statement to understand what they believe and teach.

Polluted People

All of us categorize the people in our lives from those who matter the most to us to those who matter the least. You have social circles surrounding you: immediate family, close relatives, close friends, neighbors, coworkers, and casual acquaintances. There are social circles which include people who influence you. You also have social circles which include people whom you influence.

> **Not everyone in your life wants to see you succeed.**

Polluted People want you to be like them. They want you to join their misery and their misfortunes. They want you to live by their polluted standards. Therefore, they will do all that they can to keep you contained and contaminated by their corruption.

Consider the illustration of crabs in a barrel. Some of the crabs try to escape from the barrel to freedom. But just as one crab reaches the rim of the barrel, with his escape assured, his fellow-crabs reach up and pull him back down. You have friends, family, and acquaintances that are not ready for you to escape. Believe it! Deal with it! There are people, no matter how close they are to you, who no longer fit in your new life. Do not make room for them. Remove all traces of the Polluted People from your life, not only physically, but also on all social media platforms (Facebook, Twitter, Instagram, Google+ and all of your contact lists). Do it today!

Polluted Paraphernalia

Back when I was a drug addict, I had certain items on hand to help me get high. Drug paraphernalia such as: ZigZag rolling papers, smoke pipes, bongs, roach clips, coke spoons, mirrors & razors. The best way to define paraphernalia is tools of the trade or items used to accomplish a task. Therefore, Polluted Paraphernalia are those tools from your past that are still on hand and available to help you go back to an addicted life.

I'm not saying you still have a junk drawer full of drug paraphernalia. But, what things from your past life are still lingering? What stuff is still hanging around? It might be old T-shirts (especially the ones with the marijuana leaf), old CDs or DVDs, old posters or artwork, old books or incenses. Polluted Paraphernalia serve as reminders of past addictive activities. The problem is that they also can serve as tools available to return to those past addictive activities. The time has come to dump the tools of your past pollution.

Polluted Pressures, Polluted People, and Polluted Paraphernalia - the Refiner has helped you to create a life where those things do not fit. The great thing is that He will help you to be your own Personal Environmental Protection Agent. He will help you to control your environment. He does this by helping you to replace the pollution with purity. After all, He is the Refiner!

Pure Pressures – Empower your Character

Pure People – Challenge your Thinking

Pure Paraphernalia – Enable your Actions

Now let's create your own Personal Environmental Protection policies (PEP).

Action Step 1

1. Make a list of Polluted Pressures: the music, movies, television, negative talk, etc.
2. Make a list of Polluted People: negative family members, friends, neighbors, coworkers, etc.
3. Make a list of Polluted Paraphernalia: things that represent your past addictive life.
4. For each item on your three lists - Pressures, People, Paraphernalia - identify a replacement.
5. Replace Polluted Pressures with Pure Pressures: beautiful music, movies, television, etc.
6. Replace Polluted People with Pure People: successful people, teachers, mentors, etc.

7. Replace Polluted Paraphernalia with Pure Paraphernalia: tools of your success.
8. Use these first three lists to help you identify the pollutants that need to be removed and replaced. Use the last three lists to help you establish your Personal Environmental Protection policies you can use to monitor and reinforce your development.

My Story

I never fully realized how invisible I was when I was addicted to drugs. I lived in an underground culture shunned by the rest of society. Most companies were not hiring druggies. Most churches, mosques, and synagogues wanted nothing to do with us scoundrels. Schools simply tolerated us as long as tuitions were paid and grades were passable. We were the freaks of society.

For me, the military didn't even want me. I was classified 4F, deemed undesirable, unfit to serve. You know that's pretty bad, to be rejected by the US Army at the very height of recruitment for the Vietnam War. To be fair, in my case, the Army made a good decision. I was more interested in shooting drugs than in shooting a weapon. I left the draft physical at the base in South Boston and headed back to the underground; back to invisibility.

I always felt like I was on the outside looking in. I tended to gravitate to the other outcasts and outsiders around me. Most times, they, too, were alcoholics or drug users. No one stood out in that crowd. We were all content to be invisible and to be left alone.

Of course, there was the occasional encounter with the police, which meant being chewed up and digested by the beast, AKA, the criminal-justice system. Talk about being underground, invisible, and out of sight! That was one trip that none of us wanted to deal with, but all too many street soldiers fell in the government's War on Drugs. That meant lengthy prison sentences.

NOTE: For those of you who are now incarcerated, understand that no matter how bleak your circumstances, there are no walls that can imprison you tighter than addictions. A lengthy prison sentence will demoralize your mind, but addictions destroy your everlasting soul. **The Refinement Process** can help you to be free anywhere, especially in prison.

Miraculously, I avoided arrest and incarceration; no jail or prison time for me. My personal prison did not have iron bars. I was a prisoner to my addictions. For me, coming through The Refinery was like finally being released from a life sentence. I've heard ex-convicts, upon release from prison, talk about "breathing free-air." I felt like even the air smelled fresher upon my deliverance from my addictions.

I came through **The Refinement Process**. The time was at hand for me to face a world that had not seen or known me. I was coming up from the underground, up to the surface. I was reemerging into a normal world which I forgot existed. How was I to function in this world without my old "crutch", without my old "stabilizers", my old "friends"? For me, it felt like coming out from under a heavy fog or dark cloud, into the bright sunshine.

Successful Living Through Refinement

Before you begin a course of action, always find out what the Refiner wants you to do. Ask Him for guidance. If you try to get results based on your own limited understanding, then you will get limited success. You need the understanding of the Lord, your Refiner, to achieve success without limits.

Trust in the LORD with all your heart, And lean not on your own understanding. In all your ways acknowledge Him, and He shall direct your paths. Proverbs 3:5-6 (NKJV)

To live a successful life you will need guidance and direction that exceeds your own understanding. Gaining these can be frightening and unnerving because you might think that in order to succeed you have to have all the answers. But, that is your old, faulty way of thinking, and it couldn't be farther from the truth. To succeed, you need a new and improved way of thinking. The previous verse holds the key. Do not lean on your own understanding; acknowledge Jesus, the Refiner, and He will direct your successful path.

Successful living through Refinement requires you to know what to do, to know how to do it, and then to do it. If you don't know what to do or how to do it, you cannot succeed. So, you might ask, "How do I get the answers?" You get the answers when you ask the Refiner. James 1:5 (MSG) states, *If you don't know what you're doing, pray to the Father. He loves to help. You'll get his help, and won't get condescended to when you ask for it.*

God will talk to you and give you help.

Most praying people know how to talk to God. They regularly load Him up with their To Do Lists and their Wish Lists; "Lord, I need this," or, "Lord, do this for me." Very few people know how to listen to God. He really does want to talk to you; and better than that, He wants to talk *with* you!

Let's take another Action Step and see how to apply this truth. I call it, **Inquiring of the Lord**. In order to make the most of this Action Step, you must first realize that you can talk to the Refiner and He will talk to you. Prayer is not meant to be a monolog (one person talking), it is supposed to be a dialog (two people holding a conversation). All throughout the Scriptures you can see where God listened to and replied to His people. He held conversations with ordinary people. He wants to know your thoughts and He wants you to know His thoughts.

Action Step 2

Here are seven questions that can change your life. Actually, the questions will not change your life - but, the answers to these questions and your application of these truths can absolutely change your life

Spend some quiet, uninterrupted time with the Lord. Find a place where you will not be disturbed. Take with you a pen and paper (or a recording device) to jot down the answers. Plan on spending at least 60 minutes (don't tell me that's too long, it's the length of your favorite television program). Now ask the Lord each of these questions and expect Him to answer you.

1. What do You want to say to me; what would You have me to know?
2. You have a good purpose for me; what do You want me to know about it?
3. You have a good plan for my life; what do You want me to know about it?
4. What hinders my relationship with You and how do I deal with those things?
5. Is there anyone that I need to forgive, just like You forgave me? Help me to forgive.
6. What are my wrong beliefs that You want me to be aware of? What is the truth that You want me to replace them with?
7. How can I begin to redeem the wasted years of my life, beginning today?

Be patient. This will take time and it should not be rushed. Relax and talk to the Lord the same way that you talk with your best friend. Listen to what He says and write it down. Once you have received answers to each question, begin to find ways to apply these truths to your daily life. This is an amazing process and you should make it a regular part of your relationship with the Refiner. Make this a lifelong practice; let this develop into a good habit throughout your life. It is thrilling to know that the Lord, your Refiner, hears and personally responds to you.

Recently I met Rose Goode. Let's see how Rose reemerged from living at the bottom of the pit to rising to the top of the world.

The Rose Goode Story

My name is Rose and I grew up in Chicago, Illinois, the third child of eventually eight children. My mom remarried when I was 8 years old and my step-father helped raise my mom's six children and their own two. He worked two jobs so that my mom could be at home. They taught us about Christ and we went to church and had Bible classes in our home. Each week, if we learned a Bible verse, we were rewarded an addition to our allowances.

I didn't see my natural father for eighteen years. He was an alcoholic and my mom's parents kept him away from us. When I finally found him, he was in a nursing home. The whole experience was bittersweet. It was sweet being reunited with Dad whom I loved, but I was bitter with my grandparents because they robbed me of knowing my Dad. He died in the nursing home.

I had a child, Harry, when I was 15 years old. With the loving support of my family, I managed to finish high school. Later, I was blessed with a beautiful daughter, Trish, and my little man, Jermaine. I finished cosmetology school and became a licensed hairdresser, working in a very prosperous beauty salon. Unfortunately, everybody who worked there sold drugs. So, I, too, began selling drugs, at first, just for extra money, but, eventually, I began using them.

I was 29 years old when I started using drugs. By then, my children were older. I started experimenting with cocaine after work. Although I did smoke marijuana from time to time, coke became my main thrill.

After work on Saturday nights, we'd close the shop, and everybody would start getting high. I didn't really know much about using coke until then. Those were my first experiences; getting high with my co-workers. What started on a social basis soon became a drug habit. Quickly, I went from a drug user to a drug abuser to a drug addict. At first I thought I could quit at any time, but soon I realized I needed the coke and I couldn't stop using it.

My husband was tired of my drug activities, so when his company offered him the opportunity to relocate, he took it. I suppose he thought the move might be a fresh start for our troubled marriage and a chance for me to kick my habit. Actually, I had stopped using cocaine before I moved from Chicago, although I was still smoking weed. He moved our family, 18 year old Trish and 9 year old Jermaine, to Rochester, NY. Unfortunately, I brought my addiction along with me. My daughter suspected that I got high, my younger son was unaware.

Life dramatically changed in January of the year after our move. I was involved in a car accident with my boyfriend. Yes, I was married *and* I had a boyfriend. I was a promiscuous woman, often cheating on my husband. The day of the accident I started using cocaine again. It quickly overtook me; I just picked up where I had left off. It wasn't long until I left my husband because he was threatening to take my young son away from me if I didn't stop using drugs. Even with the threat of losing Jermaine, I continued to get high.

But, I considered myself blessed because I was raised in a Christian home. Even during my darkest days, deep inside of me I could hear my mother's voice saying, *when you get tired of that lifestyle just let me know and I will help you.*

I never really abandoned my family. They all knew I was getting high. I didn't like to come around them because I couldn't hide from them the stupid, drugged-out look on my face. At family gatherings, I would always hideout in another room, too ashamed to be with them. Many times my sister, Wilma, would peek in the room to check on me, or she would bring me a plate of food. My family always said that they couldn't tell the difference in my appearance. You see, I was a hair stylist, so I could always fix myself up, my hair and makeup; I had lots of nice clothes, so I could dress up nice, but inside I was tore up and I didn't feel beautiful.

Lack of money was never an issue for me because I continued to work and I sold drugs on the side; and because I sold drugs, I was never without them. The low point for me was when I realized that I had stopped caring for my children. My son was shuffled off between my sisters who cared for him. I didn't want him to see me in the constant drugged-out state that I was in. I felt alone, really alone.

One day I had been getting high all day, well into the night. I think I must have passed out. I remember waking up the next morning and going into my bathroom where there was a full-length mirror. When I looked into the mirror I saw something that really scared me. I saw my hopeless condition; my neck was sunken in and I had a weird expression on my face. Right then and there I knew ***I need help!***

I picked up the phone and called my mother in Chicago.

"Mommy, I'm dying. I really need help."

"Rose," she said, "you are not dying because you are talking to me. Call your sister Wilma."

Wilma had always told me that when I needed help, she knew of a place which could help me. When I called her she told me to wait right there; she was on her way over. She had keys to my house to let herself in. When she arrived, she called the rehabilitation center and made an appointment for me to come in. Then she reassured me.

"Don't worry Rose, Mommy is coming. She will be flying in later today."

With their encouragement, I went to the evaluation. From there I was transferred into an in-patient drug treatment facility. During my time there, I began to remember about God and I cried out to Him. I asked Him to help me overcome my drug addiction. God helped me understand what the drugs were actually doing to me, physically, mentally and emotionally.

I did everything that was required of me at the Parkridge Treatment Center. After several weeks, my family came and met with the counselors and me. It was determined that because of my improved cooperation and tremendous support from my family I would be released ahead of schedule. The rest was up to me.

I was discharged into an eight week out-patient program. On the day of my discharge, I was really nervous. My sister came to pick me up.

"Sis, I'm really scared!" I told Wilma.

She said, "Rose, just do what they told you. Just change the people, places and things. And, by the way, things have already changed. I moved you in with me."

"Are you serious?"

"Yes. I will take you by your old place so you can clean it up. You can also pick out some personal things that you need."

When I arrived at my old apartment Mommy met us there. Of course they had found my old stash of coke. It still had some monetary "value" on the streets.

"So, what're you going to do with that?" Mom asked pointing to my coke bag.

Before I could reply, she said, "It's empty. We flushed everything down the toilet!"

I cried. They cried too. At first I cried tears of regret; after all, that was a lot of my money going down the toilet. Soon afterward I cried tears of remorse and relief. My drug burden was lifted. I think flushing away the drugs saved my life. Now I had a real chance at recovery at Wilma's place. It meant a lot to me because it showed she trusted me not steal from her.

I started going back to church where I really started to connect back to my spirituality. I knew that it was the grace of God which kept me from killing myself or overdosing. I remember one day going to a revival service at my sister's church. The guest speaker was a young woman with whom I had grown up. We had not seen each other for many years. She did not know about my history of drug addictions. When she made the altar call (that is when people go forward in the church to repent of their sins or renew their dedication to the Lord), she called my name.

She said, "Rose, come here."

As I stood before her, she said, "You've been through the storm. But, I tell you, the storm is over."

That very day I received Christ back into my life. He did a powerful work in me! I was delivered from drug addiction. It was by God's grace that I no longer physically craved drugs. From that day I was changed by the supernatural power of God.

Today, I have been clean for 26 yrs. I have no desire to use drugs again. When I was set free from the drugs, I realized that my addictions were not only to drugs; there were other areas of my life that needed fixing. I still had some character defects that needed to be addressed. Ever since I gave my life to Him, I am a new creation in Christ; old things gradually passed away, new and better things took their place. I can say I am happy. I am an active member of my church. I am reunited with my children and my family.

Rose's advice: First, you have to admit that you have a problem. Second, you have to seek help. And most important, seek God. Open up your heart to Him; He is a very present help. He will keep you.

The Refiner's Benefit Package

In your Reemergence, always remember that it was the Refiner who rescued, redeemed, and refined you. The Refiner will continually give you direction. He will daily give you His benefits.

Bless the LORD, O my soul, and forget not all his benefits Psalms 103:2

Psalm 103:3-5 lists a personal Benefits Package for those who make the Refiner Lord of their lives. These six benefits are promised to you.

The Refiner:
1. Forgives All my Iniquities
2. Heals All my Diseases
3. Redeems my Life from Destruction
4. Crowns me with Loving-kindness & Mercies
5. Satisfies my Mouth with Good Things
6. Renews my Youth

These are benefits which nobody can take away from you. Recognize that there will always be sin, sickness, and death in this world (into each life some rain must fall), but, your personal Benefits Package puts you at an advantage over every sin, sickness, and disease (anything that would come against you to destroy you). These benefits give you an assurance that the Refiner raises you up and esteems you, making sure you have all you need to reemerge in this world as a new creation. Make note of your personal Benefits Package; write it and post it in a place where you are continually reminded of His promises to you. It will give you confidence as you live your new drug-free life.

From this Reemergence Station, you are prepared to go out into this world and make a difference. The difference you make in this world will bring glory, honor, and pleasure to the Refiner.

> **The Refiner not only purifies you,**
> **He perfects you.**

Now that you have been refined (purified and perfected), live your life to the fullest. Set new goals or resurrect past goals that got derailed over the years. Go out and tell others about **The Refinement Process**. Tell them about what the Refiner did for you. Remember to give the Lord all the credit for your refinement.

Reemergence Review Platform

The butterfly does not go back to the cocoon out of which it came. The butterfly does not associate with caterpillars.

It is wiser to change your surroundings than to let your surroundings change you.

Not everyone in your life wants to see you succeed.

Polluted Pressures – Defile your Character
Polluted People – Corrupt your Thinking
Polluted Paraphernalia – Disable your Actions

Pure Pressures – Empower your Character
Pure People – Challenge your Thinking
Pure Paraphernalia – Enable your Actions

Remember the Refiner's Benefit Package (found in Psalms 103:1-5)

The Refiner not only wants to purify you, He wants to perfect you.

Relapse Road

The LORD upholds all who fall, And raises up all who are bowed down.
Psalms 145:14 (NKJV)

Relapse Road is not a narrow, unpaved path. It is a broad, smooth, well-lit street. It is the way that leads back to the bondage of addiction. It is not hidden away, far from view. It is a major thoroughfare. It runs right alongside Main Street. I know, because I was on it. And if you are not cautious, you will find yourself there, too. Relapse Road runs right past The Refinery.

The Refiner also knew that an enemy would construct his road close to The Refinery. Therefore, the Refiner took steps to insure that you would be well protected and safe. You see, you are a finished work; you are His Masterpiece! So He put certain safeguards in place to help keep you secure and successful.

After achieving so great a victory as your refinement, you will still be tempted to set foot on Relapse Road. Some of you will avoid the temptation and go on to live successful lives. Some of you will surrender to the temptation and stumble on to Relapse Road. That is what happened to me; I stumbled and fell back. It can happen, but do not despair.

We all want progress, but if you're on the wrong road, progress means doing an about-turn and walking back to the right road; in that case, the man who turns back soonest is the most progressive. C.S. Lewis

My Story

Not long after my relocation from Boston to Rochester, I was tempted to get high. Despite my recommitment and my vows to never use drugs again, I relapsed. It began with a phone call.

"Hey man, I just got back in town." It was the familiar voice of my childhood friend, Dean.

"Hey Bro', what's up?" I asked hesitantly.

"Not much, why don't you come over to my place. I got some good stuff!"

"Well, man, I don't know. Things have changed for me"

"What kinda things changed? You still down with us guys?"

"Listen, I'll come over, but I'm telling you things have changed with me. I'm not getting high like that anymore."

"Ok. That's cool. Come over anyway…we'll see."

In a moment of weakness, I totally ignored the warning signs. I went over to Dean's place. As I entered his apartment, I was hit with the old familiar smell of cannabis smoke. Dean was already lit up. The whole scene was more than I could resist. Before I knew it, I was holding in giant gulps of smoke. Feeling the euphoria of the high was not unpleasant; however, I soon realized I was back to my old form. There I was on Relapse Road.

I immediately felt a wave of guilt wash over me. Although it was great seeing my friend again, it came at too great a price. I made some lame excuse and left his place, angry with myself that I was so easily tempted and had fallen.

Several weeks later, with Christmas quickly approaching, I was again faced with temptation. To supplement my income, I worked as a part-time salesman at a fashionable men's clothing store. One night, as the shoppers gradually departed and my work shift was drawing to a close, I began preparing to close up and clean up the store. I turned off the neon signs and began closing out the cash register. Mike, my manager, approached me, "Hey, Ron, plan on sticking around after we close up. I have a little Christmas treat for the staff."

Once we closed up, cashed out the till, and cleaned up the place, Mike came out to the front counter with a couple bottles of champagne and a big plastic bag of weed.

"Come on everybody, let's party!"

"Hey, Mike, I gotta go, my girlfriend is having some friends and family over to her place."

"You can't leave us now. The party is just getting started. Besides, you worked hard, you deserve some fun."

"Well, I guess I could have some champagne."

As any teenage Casanova knows, alcohol has a way of lowering one's resistance. After a couple of glasses of the bubbly, you guessed it; it was time to fire-up some weed. My lungs ached from the pungent smoke that I captured and held tightly. Before I realized it, the few minutes I had intended to stay had turned into an hour. Once again, I had fallen.

"Hey, Mike, I really gotta go. Merry Christmas to all and to all a goodnight!"

I rushed out of the store but there was no making up the lost time and my lost sense of confidence that I had kicked my drug addiction. Frustration and thoughts of failure crowded my drugged out mind as I raced across town to Marva's apartment. Even though I rushed to get to her place, I was slow about entering once I arrived.

The sounds of music and laughter crept into the hall outside her apartment, but I was in no merry mood. Guilt and shame filled my heart as I sat on the landing outside her door.

How can I face her? I thought. *Maybe she'll just think that I'm drunk.*

Knowing that I couldn't stay out in the hall, I knocked and entered. I greeted everyone, but as soon as I made eye contact with Marva, she knew something was different. For a person who had never gotten high, Marva was very perceptive. She saw through my drunkenness and spotted my drug induced high. Her expression told me my cover was blown.

The disappointment I saw in her face that night was the final straw for me. After the party, when we were alone, I confessed to her my trespass. Tears rolled down my cheeks as I honestly repented to her and to the Refiner. She eventually forgave me, but most of all, the Refiner forgave me and gave me a fresh start.

That was the last time I ever used drugs to get high! At last, I fully realized I was rescued and refined. Finally, I recognized what Marva had been telling me from the very beginning, I could have the drugs or I could have her, but I could not have them both. I desperately wanted Marva; as desperately as I once wanted drugs. Now drugs no longer fit in my life. That space is reserved for the people and things which really matter to me. Hallelujah!

Sign Posts on Relapse Road

Just like any major street, there are many signs posted on Relapse Road.

Street Signs: Generally posted on each corner to identify the name of the street on which you are traveling and all cross streets. On Relapse Road, you are continually reminded where you are. Just look up at each intersection, there is a sign, **Relapse Road**. Your head and your heart continually remind you, *this is not where I want to be.*

Caution Signs: Posted to warn travelers of possible dangers along the way, such as: Construction Ahead, Slippery Pavement, Detour Ahead, and Do Not Pass. On Relapse Road, the caution signs were placed there by the Refiner (against the strong objections of our enemy, Satan). Wrong Way! Do Not Enter! Take Next Exit! These signs are reminders that where you are heading is extremely dangerous and disastrous. These signs are not to be ignored!

No Parking Signs: Posted to indicate that there is no space for you to pull over and pause. This street is too busy, with too much traffic. Do not interfere with the flow of traffic. Do not park here, keep moving! That is what Satan wants from you. No Parking, No Standing, just keep moving on Relapse Road.

On Relapse Road there are two signs that are sure indicators of an unsuccessful future and a disastrous destiny. The signs are **One Way** and **Dead End**. The One Way sign is an arrow which points the way to your destruction. The Dead End sign indicates that at the end of this road, there is death and destruction.

*The thief comes only to steal and kill and destroy...*John 10:10a (NIV)

The two signs you will not see on Relapse Road are **Speed Limit** and **STOP**. The enemy knows that if you slow down or even stop, then you might realize that you are heading for disaster. He wants you to continue farther and farther down this road as fast as you can. No slowing and no stopping there!

No matter how far you go down Relapse Road, there is always a sign that points to The Refinery. The door to the Repentance Station is always open for you. Do you see the sign? – **The Refinery**. Take that turn, my friend, and go back in. The Refiner is always available to bring you back.

> **You are never too far gone that you cannot repent and be rescued once again**

I know, it happened for me. Twice I relapsed, but I recognized that I could be refined anew. He welcomed me back. He refined me once again. The last time, FOREVER! You will never be out of the reach of the Refiner. He will always take you back and give you a fresh start.

Triggers, Traps, Temptations and Triumphs

A gun cannot fire unless you pull the trigger. The traps are continually baited and setup for your arrival. Temptations will try to invade the eye-gate and the ear-gate of your heart. But, you have access to a supernatural power which will cause you to triumph. It is your higher, greater power.

Temptations, when we meet them at first, are as the lion that roared upon Samson; but if we overcome them, the next time we see them we shall find a nest of honey within them. John Bunyon

Curiosity Killed the Cat, It Can Harm You Too

Curiosity is a powerful mental force. It can motivate you to seek out positive, uplifting things or negative, unrighteous things. For me, it was usually the latter. I could always tell when I was being tempted to go astray and sin. It was when I was curious about something that God told me was off-limits.

When God, through His Word of instruction and correction, sets a limit, it is for our protection. In this sinful world there are many baited traps and many slippery slopes. They are ingeniously placed by our enemy to cause us to fail. We are safe as long as we stay inside the boundaries which God places around us.

Satan uses curiosity to get you to question and eventually doubt God's Word. It always starts with a question, followed by a suggestion of a better way (not God's Way). You can see an example of this in the Bible when the serpent in the Garden of Eden used deception against the woman, Eve. He baited the trap with curiosity. You can see this exchange in Genesis 3:1-5.(NLT)

One day he asked the woman, "Did God really say you must not eat the fruit from any of the trees in the garden?" (That was his question which raised her curiosity).

"Of course we may eat fruit from the trees in the garden," the woman replied. "It's only the fruit from the tree in the middle of the garden that we are not allowed to eat. God said, 'You must not eat it or even touch it; if you do, you will die.'"

"You won't die!" the serpent replied to the woman. "God knows that your eyes will be opened as soon as you eat it, and you will be like God, knowing both good and evil." (That was his suggestion of a better way).

And with that questioning and suggesting, the seed of curiosity was planted in Eve. The Bible says *she was deceived*. She looked upon the tree and the forbidden fruit with a curious new desire to taste it. She ate it and gave it to Adam to eat. Curiosity won the day.

Satan uses curiosity to lure you into lusting for things which will defeat and destroy you. Through curiosity, the enemy attempts to lure you to go outside of God's protective boundaries. When he succeeds, and you stray off limits, it is called a *trespass*. Unrighteous curiosity can be the onramp to Relapse Road.

Do not let curiosity get you off track. Turn your curiosities toward the things of the Refiner. He will protect you and cause you to triumph.

A man may imagine things that are false, but he can only understand things that are true, for if the things be false, the apprehension of them is not understanding.
Sir Isaac Newton

Action Step

Get for yourself a Commitment Reminder that you can wear. You might choose a ring, a bracelet, a medallion or a pendant. Wear it every day. Every time you wear it, let it be a reminder to you that you are committed to the Refiner, to **The Refinement Process**, and to yourself. The Commitment Reminder is NOT a good luck charm, amulet or talisman. It has NO power, so don't treat it like anything other than a reminder.

False Justifications

One of the most powerful weapons in Satan's arsenal is deception. Whereas the truth shall make you free, deception shall entangle and enslave you. Whenever the enemy can get you to forget the truth and embrace the lie, he has deceived you; once deceived, you are headed for a fall.

Lucifer's fall from heaven began with self-deception. He mistakenly believed he could establish his throne higher than God's throne. Adam and Eve's fall from grace began with deception. They mistakenly believed that when they ate the forbidden fruit they would be like God. By the way, they were already like God; He had already created them in His image and likeness! Deception is also the belief that you are doing something right, when in reality, the thing you are doing is wrong.

On Relapse Road, the deception the enemy uses is through false justifications. Justification is the action of showing something to be right or reasonable. Therefore, false justification is the action of showing something to be right or reasonable, when in reality, it is false. In the case of relapse, the false justifications can be stated as follows:

Well, I already failed, so I might as well keep going this way.

Once an addict, always an addict!

There is no hope for me. I'll never change.

Nothing could be further from the truth! Let's explode each of these false justifications with the true justifications of God's Word:

For a just man falleth seven times, and riseth up again… Proverbs 24:16a

Therefore, if anyone is in Christ, he is a new creation; old things have passed away; behold, all things have become new. 2 Corinthians 5:17 (NKJV)

The steps of a good man are ordered by the LORD, And he delights in his way. Though he fall, he shall not be utterly cast down; For the LORD upholds him with his hand. Psalms 37:23-24 (NKJV)

Satan's purpose of false justifications is to keep you on Relapse Road forever. Do not be deceived! Get off Relapse Road and get back to The Refinery. It is always open and available for you.

My friend Craig Gause was no stranger on the Relapse Road. In fact, he was a real Relapse Road Warrior. Let's see how Craig got off the Relapse Road.

The Craig Gause Story

I heard sobbing on the receiver when I answered the late-night phone call. It was my daughter, Jessica.

"Daddy, he's gone!"

What do you mean, he's gone? Was he arrested?"

"No, Daddy, Craig Jr. is dead."

With those words I dropped to the lowest of low points in my life. Just days earlier I had enlisted my grown son, Craig Jr., to join me in operating a new restaurant. He was an up and coming rapper and a recovering alcohol and drug abuser. He was coming to town the next day. But, on that fateful night, he was the victim of a fatal car roll-over accident in which he sustained traumatic head injuries. The news of my son's tragic death sent me to the bottom of the bottle and then back to my crack pipe. My life was becoming unraveled.

My story starts in Brooklyn, NY, where I grew up in a single-parent family. My mother, Edna Mae, saw to it that I was well cared for. My father visited on weekends. As a child, I wanted to be a policeman. But my dreams of becoming a cop faded the day I saw the big cargo ships coming into the harbor; I knew then, I wanted to be a sailor.

At 17, I quit school and joined the Merchant Marines. I sailed the Mediterranean Sea, the Atlantic and Pacific Oceans, and all around the Caribbean islands. I started boozing onboard and at the various seaports. I quickly developed an alcohol addiction. I continued as a merchant seaman for a number of years, working in various roles. I moved up in the ranks, eventually becoming a Chief Cook.

Many of the sea routes took me to South America. There, I developed a taste for cocaine. My regular pattern was to buy weed in Panama, Peru, Ecuador or Bolivia. Columbia became my market to buy coke. From port to port, for me, life was one big party: food, booze, weed, women, and coke. Snorting and smoking was my thing.

I became an expert at smuggling drugs for my personal use. The Port Authorities routinely inspected incoming ships for contraband. They would bring drug-sniffing dogs and monkeys on board to find illegal drugs. I had a secret place to stash my drugs to avoid detection. My secret place – the freezers, inside the frozen turkeys! The dogs never found it. I always had superior cocaine. Unlike my friends, whose coke had been stepped on, my stash was the pure stuff.

I finally realized that I was hooked when I would only take assignments on ships that were going to South America. I would only go to the ports where I could supply my cocaine addiction. It could be the worst rust-bucket ship in the fleet, but if it was sailing for Columbia or Peru, I wanted that assignment.

By then, back in Brooklyn, I was married and had two children, Jessica and Craig Jr. My wife was not aware of my drug addictions. I had clever ways to hide them from her. My secret addictions were finally revealed when the Coast Guard called my house to notify me that I had failed the mandatory drug test. From that point, my house of cards came crashing down around my wife and kids and me. I quickly lost my good paying job.

When my unemployment benefit checks ran out, I started stealing. I pawned my wife's jewelry. It got so bad that I even took my kids' gifts from under the Christmas tree and sold them for crack. I was flooded with feelings of shame and regret; I couldn't stand it. Soon after that, I checked myself into a drug rehab program.

I did well in rehab, but I began to realize that alcohol was a trigger for my drug use. Over the years, my addictions were sporadic. I would be clean for months, sometimes years, but when I started drinking, I would get a taste for crack. Again, I relapsed. This time I lost my wife and family. She took the kids and left me.

Alcoholics Anonymous and Narcotics Anonymous helped, but I did not follow through. I felt like I was on a roller coaster. Three rehabs, three relapses, ups and downs. There came a point where I considered suicide. My plan was to drink some Drano, but I was able to pick myself up again and regain my sobriety. I eventually relocated to Conway, South Carolina.

The untimely death of my son sent me into a grief so strong that I spent days in deep depression. Countless hours I sat in my darkened room watching videos of my son performing rap songs. I returned to binge drinking, which, in turn, triggered my return to my *medicine* – crack cocaine.

Over the following months, I recognized the pattern of my life repeating itself. I knew I needed help. I turned to a Christian residential rehab program, Teen Challenge; don't let the name mislead you, it is open to all age groups. The only problem for me was that it would be two weeks before they would have room to admit me.

I decided that I would detox and tough it out until I could get into the program. Daily, I began praying and reading my Bible. It was a constant battle, but I was winning. I was determined to enter Teen Challenge clean. I even threw away my expensive crack pipe.

Then came a knock on my front door. There stood Miranda (name-changed). For months, I had been pursuing her, but she never gave me the time of day. She had three big rocks (crack) and a fifth of vodka. She was dressed for an intimate night of partying. Temptation looked good, smelled good, but she offered the very thing which I was fighting to avoid. It was crunch time for me!

"Hi, Craig. Ready to party?"

"Miranda, I can't do this. I already quit drinking and smoking. I don't do that anymore."

"What? You don't want none of this?"

"No girl, I'm through with it."

"Humph! Well, at least let me borrow your stem."

"I threw it away this morning. Goodbye." I closed the door on that old life.

With that she turned, got in her car, and drove out of my driveway and out of my dreams. I won the battle. The very next day, I got the call from Teen Challenge and left home to enter their rehab program, sober and clean.

With Teen Challenge, at last I found an effective recovery program that reintroduced me to my Savior, Jesus Christ. For the first time in many years, I learned about the supernatural power of the Lord, and my life was changed forever.

Today, I am sober and clean. I now live a life surrendered to the Lord. Day by day, He helps me stay on track. He helps me cope with the grief that I still experience due to the tragic death of my son.

Craig's advice to addicts: Stop right away. Get in touch with Jesus, the Lord, because you need help. You can't do it by yourself.

Craig's numerous travels down Relapse Road ended when he discovered the entrance to the Repentance Station. If you are struggling with your own relapse, be encouraged. The Refiner always leaves the door open to The Refinery. Enter in. Be rescued and refined.

Fallen, But Not Flattened

If you do fall, you do not have to stay fallen. We fall down, but we get up again. Remember the Refiner's promise, **For a just man falls seven times, and rises again.** It does not surprise Him when you fall. Toddlers fall many times until they learn to balance themselves and walk. Just keep getting up. If you fall, do not allow yourself to be flattened. GET UP!

It is extremely important that you not linger or loiter on Relapse Road. The quicker you exit, the quicker you can be rescued, restored and refined. There are some things to recognize whenever you fall.

Take some time to reflect and recognize:

Where am I? – You are on Relapse Road, returning to your past life of addictions.

How did I get here? – You were deceived and tempted. You believed the deception and you succumbed to the temptation.

How do I get out of here? – You must go back to the Repentance Station, repent and be restored. Leave your guilt, shame, and anger behind; be refined once again.

Recommendations to Avoid Relapse Road

Read the Holy Bible daily.

Regularly attend a Bible believing, Bible teaching church.

Tell people about your deliverance from addictions.

Pay it forward. Help someone else you know who is struggling with addictions.

Pray and give thanks to the Refiner, the Lord Jesus.

Join our online community on **The Refinement Process** Facebook page.

Also, join us on **TheRefinementProccess.com** webpage. Share your Refinement story and read stories of others who are currently struggling with drug addictions.

Post encouraging comments and share the webpage with your friends on Facebook, Instagram, Twitter & Google+.

Welcome to Your New Life

Congratulations!

Welcome to your new life! I know it was not easy and it was not always pleasant, but you have successfully completed **The Refinement Process**. The Refinery gates are wide open. Step out in to an addiction-free life. You earned it. There is a vast, vibrant future that awaits you.

The Ricky Snell Story

"Ricky, you are facing a sentence of 15 years to life in prison!"

I thought I had already hit the lowest point when I heard those words from my court appointed lawyer. My whole world came crashing down around me. How had I sunk so low? My miserable life flashed before me.

When I was eight years old, my family moved from West Virginia to upstate New York. Mom worked as a domestic maid. Dad was a construction worker. We had a great, loving family.

My parents had "rent parties" as a way to raise their monthly rent money. Card playing, usually tonk, whist or spades; James Brown, Ray Charles or the Temptations on the record player; and fried fish sandwiches and plenty of booze for sale. The next mornings, my sister and I would be assigned to clean up the ashtrays, beer cans, and paper plates. Those were my first exposures to alcohol, sipping beer from half empty cans. Mom and Dad eventually separated.

Mom died suddenly from a heart attack. One year later, Dad died. My sister and I went to live with an older cousin, Eugene. Shortly after that, Eugene died in a construction accident. His older brother, Elbert, took an early discharge from the Marines to come home to care for us. Less than a year later, Elbert, who survived military duty overseas, was gunned down in the streets of his home. He died from a bullet wound to the head.

I knew that there was a God, but I could not accept that God would allow so many deaths to surround me, taking all the people whom I loved. What kind of god would do that to me?

My first experience with marijuana was in high school. I hung around with the other football players after practice, drinking malt liquor and smoking weed. I quickly progressed to psychedelics and opiates. I never thought that I would end up like the winos and druggies that loitered on the corners of Jefferson Ave.

I eventually turned to the streets to find acceptance. Pimps, whores and hustlers became my new family. They took a special interest in me, making sure that I went home at night, and making sure that I stayed in school. They did their best to "protect" me from some of the more dangerous aspects of street life.

I managed to finish high school and I went on to earn a college degree. I became what was commonly known as a "functioning addict", able to work and earn a decent wage. I always had new cars and a roll of money. But, I was never too far from my drugs. My drug of choice was cocaine. I never planned to get hooked, but coke had other plans for my life; in fact, it was desperately trying to take my young life! I lived a life of drug abuse and addictions, selling heroin to support my habit.

Growth is such a gradual thing that many times we do not see it in ourselves. Other people around us see an increase in our stature and size more readily then we see it ourselves. That is also true of our demise; others can see us slipping away due to drug abuse and addiction quicker then we see it, if we see it at all. My sister, who was like a mother figure, saw my character change long before I saw it.

My drug addictions were taking a heavy toll on my finances. I began finding dishonest ways to feed my wallet, feed my face and feed my growing coke addiction. The reality of my desperate situation became evident on the day I asked my sister for $10 to gas up my car. She gave the money to her son (not to me) and told him to go get the gasoline. I then realized that the woman who once trusted me with thousands of dollars, no longer trusted me with $10.

I stole money from relatives, which led me to stay away from my family because I didn't want them to see me in that fallen condition. My family searched the hospitals and morgues to try to find me. My family intervened, assuring me that they loved me and wanted to help me get clean. Finally, I went to rehab and stayed clean for several months, but soon afterward, I went right back to it. Again, I went back to rehab and stayed clean for 8 or 9 years; but, I eventually relapsed.

I got involved with Narcotics Anonymous. I saw some value in the 12-step ideology, but I was disillusioned by the experience. The support leaders explained that I could look to anything as my "higher power", a light bulb or a door knob, etc. Instinctively, I looked at God as my higher power, even though I didn't really know Him.

I found God at the bottom of my pit. I lost custody of my children, lost my job, and even lost my health. I was diagnosed with an aggressive cancer. It was like "going through the fire". A friend invited me to church where I found some relief. I saw such joy and peace. Although I found some hope at church, and I was even healed, my life was still out of control.

I was arrested on bank robbery charges. The whole church rallied around me with fasting and prayer. Through that Christian love and support, I came to know God's mercy and love. I knew that I could trust God to see me through some difficult years.

I faced 15 years to life. But, my newly found Lord had other plans for me. God sent ministers from church to be character witnesses and to plead with the judge for mercy, saying that the punishment was too harsh for the crime committed. My sentence was reduced to 3 years.

During my years in prison, I got serious about knowing God. I learned how to serve the Lord. I prayed and repented of my drug addictions. I asked God to take the drugs out of my life.

"Don't use, don't use, don't use!" God kept telling me, "You've got gold in your spirit!"

That was His way of telling me that He loved me and valued me. I didn't have immediate results, but I persisted in my sobriety until the Lord finally, totally delivered me from my addictions. God gave me back all that I lost through my drug addictions. I served out my prison sentence and parole. I was free from prison and free from drugs.

I am living God's perfect plan for my life. I have been refined. I now live in a nice neighborhood. I have joint custody of my younger children; I am working and studying for another college degree.

My advice to addicts: Get help. Don't stay out there too long. Addiction and the devil work together. When you fall, get back up and walk out of that mud hole. Get help, time is of the essence.

Ricky experienced a new life, and you can too. **The Refinement Process** is here to assist you in making the steps which lead to your new life. Make this process a part of your new life style. Incorporate the lessons learned here into your everyday mindset.

I believe that if you can make it through The Refinery, then you can make it through any difficulty that comes your way. Live free, my friend. Live your life to the fullest. Because of the Refiner, you can have the abundant life which He promised: Love, joy, inner peace, patience, kindness, goodness, gentleness, faithfulness and self-control.

These are called the *Fruits of the Spirit*, and every day they are all available to you.

Just know that even though you are leaving The Refinery, the Refiner is not leaving you. Jesus, the Refiner, still wants to be part of your new life. You still need to make Him a part of your new life. His promise to you is that He is as close to you as the mention of His name. Whenever you face difficulties and disasters, call on Jesus, the Refiner. He is available to help you.

With this welcome also comes warning.

Warnings for Your New Life

Beware!

Although your future is bright, you will still have challenges awaiting you on the road ahead.

Habit, if not resisted, soon becomes necessity. Augustine

Life will hand you many opportunities to fail. Hurdles, pitfalls, and traps all await you in your new life. Trials and temptations are all part of life, and, sometimes, they might get the best of you (or more likely, the worst of you).

Recognize that you have been cleansed by the Refiner. Every day you will need Him to help keep you pure. Don't let anyone sell you a bill of goods. Your new life will not always be a bed of roses. There will be times when the past will look tantalizing. There may even come a time when you succumb to your past unrighteous desires. We live in a cursed, sin-filled world, so do not be dismayed if you find yourself on Relapse Road. Whenever you fall, get up and be refined again.

My Story

As for me, the Refiner did not stop purifying me when He delivered me from drug addictions. Over the years of my new life, He caused me to identify other areas requiring His Refinement. During my young adult life, I had developed some very impure ways. For one, I had a filthy mouth; my vocabulary of profanities was vast. Second, I was used to smoking a pack of cigarettes per day. Third, I had a secret lust for pornography.

For by one sacrifice he has made perfect forever those who are being made holy. Hebrews 10:14 (NIV)

Because of my earlier progression through The Refinery and my being purified of drug addictions, the next addictions and bad habits did not require the full **Refinement Process**. Once again, I had to go through the Reflection Station and the Repentance Station. Those two powerful stations helped me to recognize my faults, admit and submit them to the Refiner's hand. One by one, the addictions and immoral practices were purged from my life.

A nail is driven out by another nail. Habit is overcome by habit. Erasmus

Gradually, Marva and others noticed my cursing and swearing ended. Literally, overnight my cigarette smoking ceased: NO nicotine gum or patches, NO hypnosis, NO behavioral modification therapy. One day I was a tobacco-smoker, the next day I no longer smoked, and I haven't smoked for over 35 years.

The secret lusts took more time; which is not the fault of The Refinery. It simply took longer for me to reflect, understand the destructive soul-ties and finally repent and receive my purification. Today, I am totally free! And you can be too!

For that reason, I firmly believe that **The Refinement Process** will work for any and all addictions: gambling, pornography, tobacco smoking, alcohol excesses, foul language, and on and on. The same five Refinery Stations, Reflection, Repentance, Redemption, Recommitment, and Reemergence, can help you to be free from anything that has control over your life. If you apply **The Refinement Process**, you will come forth as pure gold.

My refinement afforded me a long and successful career in corporate America in the field of Information Technology. Marva and I are ordained pastors, serving at Church of Love Faith Center, in

Rochester, NY under the leadership of Bishop Gregory L. Parris and his wife, Pastor Myra Parris.

I have been married to Marva, the love of my life, for 36 years. Together we have raised three wonderful children, Melvin, Elizabeth, and Ronald Jr. (Ronnie). They each, in turn, are raising the next generation of masterpieces, Chassity, Melvin Jr., Nathaniel, Aliyah, Melena, Taina, Jahmiel, Miriam, Yusuf, Lael and Ronald III (Trey).

Endnotes

---

[1] Matthew 13:45-46
[2] 1 Corinthians 13:12 (NIV)
[3] Proverbs 27:19 (NIV)
[4] Psalms 139:23-24 (NIV)
[5] 2 Samuel 12:1-7 (NIV)
[6] 2 Samuel 12:13a (NIV)
[7] Proverbs 14:12 (NKJV)
[8] 1 Corinthians 13:11 (NKJV)
[9] IBID
[10] Luke 9:33 (NKJV)
[11] Luke 9:35 (NKJV)
[12] Luke 4:18-19
[13] John 3:16-17
[14] Matthew 11:6
[15] 2 Corinthians 5:21 (NIV)
[16] Romans 12:2 (NIV)
[17] Good News Publishers, Westchester, IL

www.ingramcontent.com/pod-product-compliance
Lightning Source LLC
LaVergne TN
LVHW051604070426
835507LV00021B/2763